BOOKS BY WAYNE RICE

Far-out Ideas for Youth Groups
Fun 'N' Games
Junior High Ministry
Right-on Ideas for Youth Groups
Way-out Ideas for Youth Groups

Junior High Ministry

A GUIDEBOOK FOR THE LEADING AND TEACHING OF EARLY ADOLESCENTS

Wayne Rice

ZONDERVAN
PUBLISHING HOUSE
OF THE ZONDERVAN CORPORATION
GRAND RAPIDS, MICHIGAN 49506

Many of the games listed in chapter nine under the heading "Games and Recreation That Include Everyone" were reprinted from the book *Fun 'N' Games* by Wayne Rice, Denny Rydberg, and Mike Yaconelli (Zondervan, 1977), used by permission.

Many of the activities and ideas in chapters nine and ten were either reprinted or adapted from *Ideas* (volumes one through twenty), published by Youth Specialties, 1968-1977, 861 6th Avenue, San Diego, California 92101. Used by permission.

JUNIOR HIGH MINISTRY: A GUIDEBOOK FOR THE LEADING
AND TEACHING OF EARLY ADOLESCENTS
© 1978 by Wayne Rice

Library of Congress Cataloging in Publication Data

Rice, Wayne.
  Junior high ministry.

  Bibliography: p.
  1. Church work with youth.   I. Title.
BV4447.R45   259   78-23473
ISBN 0-310-34971-0

Printed in the United States of America

to
Marci, Nathan, and Amber

Contents

Preface

I began working with junior highers back in the fall of 1963 when I took a job as junior high club director for Ventura County California Youth for Christ. I was fresh out of high school at the time and was given the job primarily to prepare me for bigger and better things: a chance to become a high school club director. (That's where the prestige was.)

Little did I know that fifteen years and several thousand kids later, I'd still be involved in junior high ministry, and to top it off, I'd be doing a book on the subject. I did make it as a high school youth director, but somewhere along the line I guess I also got hooked on junior high kids.

This book is based on those fifteen years of experience. I have attempted to reinforce my personal experience with that of hundreds of other youth workers who have taught me a great deal over the years. I have also picked up a considerable amount of helpful information from good books and other published resources dealing with early adolescence.

It has been said that one of the best ways to learn about

something is to teach it, and I have discovered this for myself. For the past several years I have led dozens of seminars on junior high ministry as part of my work with Youth Specialties, and this has forced me to think through the finer points of junior high work and to organize my thoughts on this subject. This book is a direct result of those seminars in that many who attended asked that I put this in written form.

I have tried to be thorough, but this book is not meant to be exhaustive or the final word on junior high ministry. Nor is it intended to replace any of the fine books currently available on adolescent psychology and youth ministry. It is a look at junior high ministry from one veteran's point of view, and hopefully it will complement the work of others in this area. It covers most of the basics as I see them and is designed to stimulate and to challenge both the experienced and the inexperienced junior high worker in the Christian community. Of course, my greatest hope is that a lot of junior high kids will benefit.

For the purposes of this book, I have defined a junior higher as any young person between the ages of twelve and fifteen. Usually, that means the seventh, eighth, and ninth grades, but this material is not limited to either those ages or those years in school. We can give or take a year or so and we'd still be talking about basically the same group of kids.

In this book I refer to them most of the time as "junior highers," but for variety I also use the term "early (or young) adolescents." Occasionally I call them "kids." Some people may object because they think this sounds too young for this age group, but I have found that most junior highers use this term to refer to themselves. "Students" is another term I sometimes use; this has a nice neutral ring to it.

It is interesting, by the way, that there is no term that adequately identifies this age group. The adjectives in the terms *junior highers* and *early adolescents* imply that they are not quite high schoolers and not quite adolescents. In *The Vanishing Adolescent* Edgar Friedenberg says that if a society has no word for something, either it does not matter to them or it matters too much to talk about. Since there are more than sixteen million people in this country who are part of this "unnamed" group, the latter is probably the case here.

Another problem that has arisen in recent years to complicate the lives of people who try to write clear sentences is the controversy over the use of the sexist pronouns *he* and *she*. I share people's objections to using the masculine *he* or *him* when also referring to *she* or *her,* but I have a greater distaste for constantly using "he or she" throughout a book. I have used "he or she" when I felt it was good to do so, but most of the time I have used the traditional "he" to indicate both masculine and feminine. Hopefully, you can add your own "or she" in those cases, with my apologies.

I would like to take this opportunity to express my gratitude to a few people who have been very helpful and supportive. First, my co-workers at Youth Specialties, Mike Yaconelli and Denny Rydberg, who were not only very patient with me while I worked on this book but who also encouraged me to write it.

There were also a lot of people in junior high ministry who shared their ideas with me (like the ninety-four in chapter eight), and to all of them, a special thank-you. I will, however, single out Bill Wennerholm of Hollywood Presbyterian Church. He probably doesn't realize it, but several years ago he convinced me that junior high ministry is where the action is. You were an inspiration, Bill, and I learned a lot from you.

In addition, I probably wouldn't have written the book had it not been for the support and patience of Robert K. DeVries and the fine folks at Zondervan Publishing Company. Bob gave me the green light and then kept the pressure off.

My wife Marci never complained, even though I took up a lot of "our" time working on this book. I have dedicated it to her and to my terrific children, Nathan and Amber, who often wondered why daddy was too busy to play. I'll take this opportunity to say to them: I love you.

1
Junior High Ministry in the Local Church

This book is about young adolescents who are approximately twelve through fifteen years old. They are referred to as "junior highers" primarily because of the educational institutions they attend—junior high schools. Of course, age is seldom an accurate means for isolating a group of people into a category, but this age range was chosen because society, through institutions such as junior high schools, sees the years twelve through fifteen as a stage of life. However, having been categorized and labeled a "stage," young adolescence has then been neglected.

My objective in this book is to suggest some practical ways the Christian church can minister to junior highers more effectively. It is my conviction that ministry to junior high school students, people between the ages of twelve and fifteen, is without a doubt one of the most important and strategic ministries for the church. Hopefully, this book will help you, the junior high worker, to catch this vision and to better understand and meet the needs of early adolescents.

Usually when youth ministry is considered in the church,

the primary concern is with high school students, or with the college group, even though there may be more junior highers. It is not uncommon for a church to spend a substantial amount of money on programming and professional staff to meet the needs of senior highs without ever considering the same for its junior highers. The children's department of the church naturally concerns itself only with children up through the sixth grade, since the seventh grader is viewed as having outgrown all the old methods and is now ready for something else. The problem is that few people seem to know what that something else is. So the end result is that the junior higher is more often than not simply put on hold; we wait for him to pass through this stage and to grow up into someone to whom we are better equipped to minister.

There are many reasons why junior highers have been traditionally neglected in the church. Perhaps the most obvious one is that the vast majority of adults are afraid of junior high kids. Adults seem to be intimidated by junior highers or at least to have an acute distaste for them. Most parents that I know would be delighted if somehow their own kids were able to just by-pass the junior high years altogether.

Adults don't feel this way about older teen-agers or younger children. Senior highs appear to be, in many ways, a lot like young adults. They are somewhat predictable and are able to communicate on a more mature level. They can drive, have money, and are often willing to work and to take on many leadership responsibilities, all of which makes this youth worker's job a great deal easier. Junior highers generally offer none of the above, and this diverts many potential junior high workers into other fields.

Similarly, the prospect of working with or teaching the younger children in the church poses no real threat to the adult who wishes to serve in some way. To the youngster, the adult represents authority, knowledge, power, and deserves respect (or else!). Little kids are for the most part manageable, cute, and on top of that they believe most everything you tell them.

Not so with junior highers. Much to everyone's dismay they love to challenge authority, and they have a knack for asking disturbing questions that are often difficult to answer.

According to Don Wells, principal of the Carolina Friends School and member of the Task Force on Middle Schools (National Association of Independent Schools), junior highers are neglected by adults for the following reasons:

1) Early adolescents defy being defined, and that's irritating. We can set some hazy marks about them on a scale relative to any act, value, skill, or any other single thing, but the result is either as useful as a definitive description of all bubbles, or so definitive as to classify all bubbles, save one, the exception. And those things we can't define, can't make sound predictions about, indeed those things that even resist our efforts to classify them by the effrontery of simply being themselves, we tend to avoid. In the case of the early adolescent, we have avoided.

2) Because of our inability to define, the holder of the needed information is a child, and what adult wants to be dependent on a *child* as his resource person? Precious few it seems.

3) The number of persons who had a positive, healthy, happy early adolescence in a supportive, caring environment equals the number of adults presently whole enough to creatively and maturely identify with an early adolescent toward the goal of successful interaction. Such persons were an endangered species long before the blue whale.

4) We all have fragile egos, and we all play to the audience "out there." When we have our druthers, we pick good audiences because they tend to make us feel good. Early adolescents are very unpredictable audiences, and many times they hiss and boo. Not because they don't like you, but because they aren't sure they like themselves; not because they want to corporately hurt you, but because they aren't thinking corporately but individually; not because they understand and reject, but because they don't understand that you don't understand.

5) To appreciate the world of the early adolescent, one must "become" in the world of the early adolescent. Such

total immersion is not as necessary when working with other age groups, for we readily accept that we can never experience early childhood again and delight in our ability to enjoy, nurture, and support the childhood experience. Also, we revel in the fact that we can have "adult dialogue" with children beyond early adolescence, and although we then have to take full cognizance of their burgeoning physical and mental prowess, they do seem eminently more reasonable than they were just a few years back. Early adolescence cannot be dealt with so neatly, for it has been the stage in our lives replete with terror, anxiety, fear, loneliness, hate, love, joy, desperation, all expressed (or experienced) with the intensity of adulthood yet devoid of adult perspective. It is an age of vulnerability, and vulnerability implies potential pain; adults know that pain hurts, and they don't often willingly enter a domain in which they will be hurt. So we avoid (deny) because we as adults cannot again handle adolescence.

6) Early adolescents are easily identifiable as imperfect specimens of the human condition. They are not the epitome of anything we can define as "good" from our adult perspective. Since they aren't consistent, they can't reach perfection on our terms. We don't use positive superlatives in describing them. However, all of us generally prefer dealing with those who have "made it" in the superlative sense. Therefore, because early adolescents are moving in such constant flux, they never make it to a desirous end within that stage. Dealing with early adolescents does not afford us the satisfaction of experiencing a finished product, and we lose vision and perspective easily. (And so do they.)[1]

So for most adults, it simply boils down to the fact that junior high ministry does not appear to be a very pleasant thing to do, and most people avoid unpleasant things. Junior highers are stereotyped as being rowdy, restless, silly, impossible to handle, moody, loud, vulgar and disrespectful, and, worst of all, completely unpredictable. And all of these characteristics may be true at times. But to be completely fair, the truth is that junior highers offer more than enough to offset whatever hazards may exist in working with them. They are, for example, tremendously enthusiastic, fun, loyal, energetic, open, and, most importantly, ready to learn just as much as the creative youth worker is willing to help them learn. The personal satisfaction and sense of accomplishment that are part of working with junior highers are unequalled anywhere else.

In my experience as a professional Christian worker I have served in dozens of churches and parachurch organizations and in a variety of roles, and I have had the opportunity to work with most age groups in some way. I've run "children's church," organized summer camps, taught Sunday school classes, directed choirs, led Bible studies, preached a sermon or two, held seminars, and so on. I have to be honest and say that my preference at the present time is to work with people closer to my own age. I am, after all, an adult, not a kid, and I can identify more with adults than with kids. But having said that, I can also say with an equal degree of certainty that if I were to select the most challenging area of ministry in the church, it would have to be working with junior high kids.

I have on a number of occasions heard intelligent people state that all one can really expect to do is more or less "babysit" junior highers through their difficult years. Just keep an eye on them, keep them occupied, give them enough activity to hold their attention and wait until that glorious day when they become high schoolers; old enough for a "meaningful" ministry. To expend a great deal of effort working with junior highs is like throwing pearls before swine, or so they say. It is good stewardship of both time and money to wait until you can really do some good.

This reminds me of a rather ridiculous story about a major highway that ended at the edge of a high cliff. Hundreds of feet below were jagged rocks. For some unknown reason, day after day motorists would drive off the end of the road at full speed and plunge onto the rocks below. This situation was left unattended for some time. Well, one bright, sunny day a group of experts arrived on the scene to discuss solutions to the problem. After a considerable amount of study and after holding

committee meetings they decided to build a hospital at the
bottom of the cliff!

The real problem here, of course, is not at the bottom of the
cliff but at the top. It makes more sense to protect people from
the fall. I believe that the average junior higher stands at the
top of the cliff. Most surveys I have ever seen indicate that the
person most likely to drop out of church is the ninth grader. It
is during the junior high years that many young people decide
that they are tired of being baby-sat.

A Time of Transition

The years between eleven and fourteen are without a doubt
the most unsettling in a person's life. This is when puberty
occurs; a person changes physically, and in every other way,
from a child to an adult. During this period there is a tremendous amount of upheaval, which takes many different forms. A
once-in-a-lifetime metamorphosis is taking place. The specifics
of puberty will be described later in the book.

Puberty is not a disease that a person catches, so it doesn't
need a cure. Everyone experiences it, and so it's perfectly
normal, even though it results in what appears to be rather
abnormal behavior.

For example, it is not uncommon at all for a junior higher to
suddenly catch a case of the giggles or to erupt into tears
without warning. Or he might be bursting with energy one
moment yet for no apparent reason become lethargic and lazy
the next. He will sometimes act very much like an adult and at
other times act like a child. He may become unusually preoccupied with the mirror and worry to the point of depression
about every supposed defect in his physical appearance. He
may decide to do a certain thing one moment and then change
his mind and do precisely the opposite almost immediately;
hardly what one would call "normal" behavior. Actually, when
working with junior highers it is a good idea to keep in mind
that the abnormal *is* the normal most of the time.

For some junior highers, the new experiences and problems

they encounter during puberty will be rather mild and will go practically unnoticed by the casual observer. But for the majority of kids there is serious difficulty, and often they suffer from complete inability to cope with the pressures and demands of early adolescence. Erik Erikson writes that it is not until adolescence that the individual begins to see himself as having a past and a future that are exclusively his. Adolescence is thus a pivotal time of both review and anticipation. It is a time when the individual seeks his distinctive identity. This search consists of a conscious sense of personal uniqueness, a subconscious striving for continuity of experience, and a solidarity with group ideals.[2]

It is during these years that the child attempts to put away childish things in his quest to become a person with a unique identity, and most of these efforts result in a lot of stumbling and failure. The junior higher is for the first time trying to sever ties with the family or with established authority figures in order to gain some independence, and this always brings complications. Parents are naturally reluctant to let go, and they don't understand what is going on. Meanwhile the kids are certain that they are not being allowed to grow up and that the only possible solution is out-and-out rebellion.

During the junior high years the juvenile crime rate soars, and running away, drug use, pregnancy, and suicide are not at all uncommon. Without belaboring the point, there is more than enough evidence to show that the junior high years are uniquely troublesome, requiring more, not less, of the church's concern and attention.

A Time of Questioning

At this age the mind is also developing rapidly and most junior highers begin to call into question much of what they have been taught. Many childhood myths crumble as they discover new ways of perceiving reality. They no longer consider everything their parents or teachers tell them to be "truth"; they want to understand for themselves.

One fourteen-year-old girl describes the conflict between her old and new perspective. "I had a whole philosophy of how the world worked. I was very religious and I believed that there was unity and harmony and that everything had its proper place. I used to imagine rocks in the right places on all the right beaches. It was all very neat and God ordained it all, but now it seems absolutely ridiculous."[3]

It is not at all uncommon for junior highers to suspend temporarily or even to reject entirely the values and beliefs acquired during childhood. This continues until they are able to determine whether or not these values and beliefs have any validity for or relevance to their new young adult lives. Just as Santa Claus and the stork were discarded years earlier, so for many the God of the Old Testament and the Christ of the New Testament seem not quite as believable as they once were.

In light of this, it would seem obvious that it is dangerous for the church merely to occupy junior highers with meaningless activity as opposed to offering them thoughtful and honest answers to the questions that issue out of their emerging faith. There is certainly a danger here of losing them entirely with little chance of reaching them or ministering to them later on.

A Time of Openness

One of the primary reasons that working with junior highers can be tremendously rewarding is that these young people are very open to new ideas and to guidance. For most junior highers, the search for an identity is a complicated trial-and-error process that accounts for their characteristic unpredictability. They will accept or try things one day that they might discard the next for something completely different. They may try something new or behave in a way that coincides with their concept of how they want to be and how they want others to view them, and they may continue in it for a while or at least repeat it enough times to be sure. But if they are unsatisfied with the feedback they receive, they will likely discontinue this behavior and seek out another alternative. This is why a junior higher will enthusiastically accept something this week that he rejected last week. For the junior higher, life becomes a lot like a big jigsaw puzzle with a lot of the pieces still missing. Senior high school students, by comparison, are nearing the completion of this process and will often be extremely rigid and set in their ways. One study by the Menninger Clinic in Topeka, Kansas, found that in most cases senior highs had already adopted a permanent life style. On the other hand, junior highers remain extremely open and flexible.

A few years ago I attended my ten-year high school class reunion, which successfully brought together most of the Camarillo High School class of '63. It was good to see my old friends and classmates once again, but it was also kind of eerie. I had the strange feeling all evening that I had been put into a time machine and thrust backward to my high school days as I renewed old acquaintances and watched the action out on the dance floor. It was like being back in high school again. Everyone was so much the same. I discovered that with few exceptions I could have made very accurate predictions as to what those high school graduates would be like ten years down the road. The introverts were still introverts. The extroverts had become insurance salesmen. The high achievers had become successful in business or in education, and the class "Fonzies" were still trying to act out that role. Personalities were for the most part unchanged as well as their religious preferences.

The point is that while it is possible to make reasonably reliable predictions about high school seniors, you cannot accurately predict much about junior highers. They have not yet "set themselves in concrete," and they remain open to all kinds of possibilities.

Of course, this openness often takes the form of gullibility. The junior higher is an easy target for Madison Avenue, the rock-and-roll disc jockey, the drug pusher, or anyone selling just about anything. They are all after the soul of the junior higher, and it seems only fair that the church should be right in there too. There is no question that junior highers are trying to work out their lives and to come up with values and character traits of their own. And for some, the values of their parents, good or bad, have already been eliminated. It is doubtful that there will ever again be a more appropriate time to offer to any young person the Christian alternative.

A Time of Decision

Erik Erikson maintains that early adolescents between the ages of twelve and fifteen are not really ready to "install lasting idols or ideals as guardians of a final identity."[4] It is true that most junior highers are engaged in a fact-finding period that makes the majority of their assumptions, conclusions, and decisions rather fragile and temporary. But for some junior highers, significant decisions are possible, and they may remain operative for the rest of their lives. The celebrated novelist Ayn Rand stated on a television talk-show interview that at age thirteen she decided to become an atheist.

Junior highers will make numerous decisions and commitments, some of which may be lasting. But if their decisions are going to have any meaning at all, they must come as a result of their own reasoning, understanding, and process of elimination. They make a great many immature decisions, but they feel a sense of accomplishment by doing so. Their quest for independence causes them to make as many of the decisions that govern their lives as possible.

The temptation for the Christian junior high worker is to push for decisions—asking junior highers to make a commitment to follow Christ, to be a good witness for Christ, and the like. And usually the decision can't wait, it must be made immediately. ("Now is the accepted time. . . .") Of course, if the case for such a commitment has been communicated in an appealing way, it is likely that the junior high worker will get good results. Junior highers will usually make just as many decisions as they are asked to make.

The problem is that decisions like these are taken very

seriously in the church and are considered to be of a sacred, life-changing nature. Yet for the young adolescent, who has been put on the spot and asked to make a decision before he was ready, it has become just one more decision. If it works out, fine, but if it doesn't, then it will be soon forgotten.

I have seen posters in youth group meeting rooms that said "Not to decide is to decide." This is catchy and very motivating, but it also creates a real problem for the junior higher. There are many times when not to decide is the best thing he or she can do. Junior highers need the church's help as they attempt to gain a better understanding of the implications of the Christian commitment, but they do not need to be pushed into making a commitment. It is unfortunate that many young people are decisioned to death in the church during those junior high years; this makes a meaningful commitment less likely later on in life.

It is not our job as junior high workers to produce a large number of decisions. More times than not we fall into that trap only because we want some kind of measurable results; we want to know how we are doing. They are more for our good than anyone else's. Significant decisions will be made along the way by junior highers, but it is wise to allow these decisions to come on their own.

The junior high years offer us a unique opportunity for ministry in the local church. At no other time in a person's life are so many options considered, changes made, and lives shaped. It is not a time for baby-sitting but for caring and letting each junior higher know that he is significant to Christ, to the church, and to the world around him. Young minds and growing faiths have many questions that require honest answers. These kids are attempting to establish themselves as individuals worthy of the love of God.

Notes
[1]From an unpublished manuscript by Donald A. Wells; used by permission.

[2]Erik Erikson, *Identity, Youth and Crisis* (New York: W. W. Norton, 1968), p. 91.

[3]Jerome Kagan, "A Conception of Early Adolescence," in *Twelve to Sixteen: Early Adolescence,* ed. Robert Coles et al. (New York: W. W. Norton, 1972), p. 94.

[4]Erikson, p. 54.

2
The Junior High Worker

A friend of mine who has been involved in full-time junior high ministry for almost fifteen years once said, "If you can learn to run a junior high group, then you can rule the world." Whether or not you take him seriously, the point he was trying to make is a good one: It does take a special kind of person to work with junior high kids. If you are willing to develop the skills, patience, courage, and know-how required to work with junior highers, then anything else you want to do later on ought to be a breeze (including ruling the world, should you be so inclined).

The importance of the person or persons involved as junior high workers cannot be underestimated. The junior high worker or teacher is central to the success or failure of any program or methodology. Junior high work is essentially relational, and the people involved in it are the main ingredient.

There is an abundance of good resources, ideas, curriculum and books available for junior high programs, but the truth is that if the kids don't like or can't relate to the teacher/sponsor/youth worker in charge, then there is little chance that anything will work very well. The good news is that the reverse is also true most of the time. That is, if you are the kind of person who relates well to junior highers, and if you are able to communicate reasonably well with them, then it is quite possible that you could use almost any resource or new idea with a degree of success. This, of course, doesn't mean that the junior high worker who relates well to junior highers doesn't have to be selective about resources, but he does have a distinct advantage over the other person.

Junior highers will nearly always describe their youth programs or classes in terms of the youth worker or teacher. *They* are the ones who make the class or program great or terrible. It is interesting that high school and college students almost always select their classes by subject. They look over the course offerings and choose classes by the curriculum and subject matter. But with junior highers, there is little concern about content. The important question from one junior higher to the other is always, *"Who* did you get?" The goal is to get the good teachers and to avoid the bad ones.

Educator Edward Martin comments about this tendency to equate the teaching with the teacher:

> Curriculum reform projects of the past ten years in the academic disciplines have tried to improve schools by producing better materials, some of which could be taught by any teacher. Most of them now realize that with a bad teacher, students will feel the new course is as bad as the old. Parents, principals, and guidance counselors keep telling youngsters that it should not matter who the teacher is. They say you should be able to learn from someone you do not like. This is true only when the personal dislike is mild and is overpowered by respect for the teacher's fairness and competence. Most teachers accept the necessity of being liked by their students; some turn this into an end in itself. Students want a positive personal relationship with their teachers, but they want more.[1]

It would be convenient if everyone who was willing or

available could do the job, but unfortunately there are people who just can't be a junior high worker. What this means is that if we in the church really care about meeting the needs of our junior highers, then we should make every effort to have qualified people working with them.

And what is a qualified person?

First, a word about some "unqualifications." Take, for example, the stereotype of the junior high worker: a handsome, young, funny, athletic, single college grad who plays a guitar, owns a custom-built van with a stereo in the back, and has an apartment at the beach. Even with all these "assets," this person could be hopelessly unqualified to work with junior highers. It is possible, of course, to win the affection and admiration of junior highers for a while by being "macho," or by having musical ability, good looks, the latest clothing styles, and so on, but the majority of good junior high workers that I know possess few of these things. They really aren't necessary. That doesn't mean you cannot be young, beautiful, and talented, but you certainly don't have to be in order to relate well and minister effectively to junior highers. Kids will like you and listen to you not because you happen to be "neat" or glamorous but because you like them and listen to them.

Now on to the qualifications.

One prerequisite for working with junior highers (or any age group for that matter) in the church is spiritual maturity. I assume that anyone who takes on a position of leadership in the church has a meaningful relationship with Christ that can be communicated to others. I won't dwell on this here, but it is obviously inappropriate to have someone who does not have this basic foundation teaching or ministering to others in the church.

There are other things that would be most helpful to you when working with junior highers, such as a sense of humor, the ability to communicate, and a generous helping of patience, but there are only three *primary* qualifications that I consider essential. They are:

1. You must be able to identify with the problems, needs, and feelings of junior highers.
2. You've got to like junior highers.
3. You've got to be willing and able to give the necessary time.

Learning to Understand Them

The first qualification for a junior high worker is the ability to identify with the early adolescent; that is, to understand what it is like to be a junior higher. Most adults simply cannot do this. To most adults junior highers seem incredibly strange and impossible to understand. They are moody, noisy, unreasonable, disrespectful, irreverent, lazy, and just plain crazy most of the time, Mr. Average Adult would say. And, of course, to the casual adult observer, most of these things are more or less true. But to the junior higher, there are very good reasons behind all those idiosyncrasies that adults don't like, and they desperately want someone who will try to understand. Without this understanding, communication becomes almost impossible.

Every adult has one very good point of identification with junior highers—he or she was once upon a time a junior higher too. You and I were junior high kids not *too* many years ago. In reality, the problems that junior highers face today are not that different from the problems we faced when we were that age, so it would seem logical that we would have a certain amount of empathy almost automatically.

But psychologists tell us that there is a problem for normal adults when it comes to remembering what it was like to be an adolescent between the ages of twelve and fifteen. They call it "repression," which is sort of an adult amnesia. Repression is defined as the "rejection from consciousness of painful or disagreeable ideas, memories, and feelings." It is something that the mind does to make life more endurable—it automatically tries to forget, or at least block from memory, painful experiences of the past. Those painful experiences are never lost completely from consciousness; they are just pushed back into the recesses of the mind and never recalled. It's common for therapists to use hypnosis or some other method to help people recall and deal with repressed events.

What does all this have to do with working with junior highers? Simply that psychologists also tell us that some of life's most painful experiences occur during puberty—while you were a junior higher. Consider the embarrassment and humiliation of the struggle with parents for independence, the times when one was not accepted by the peer group, guilt feelings brought on by new awareness of one's sexuality, puzzling questions from a developing mind, love triangles and broken hearts, and the list could go on and on. No one wants to go through life with all *that* on his mind. So it is repressed. And that accounts for the average adult's inability to understand junior highers very well. They just don't remember. Says educator John A. Rice:

> . . . but where is one who does not wince at the memory of his adolescence? . . . Women say they cannot remember the pangs of childbirth. Crafty nature blots them out, lest there be no more. So also one does not remember one's second birth . . . from childhood into youth. This second birth . . . becomes in memory a dull pain.[2]

The best way for you to identify with junior highers is to get in touch with your own early adolescent years. While it may be difficult for some people to reach back and relive events and recall feelings that happened a long time ago, it is not impossible and it does wonders to help the junior high worker to empathize with kids. Your memory can be one of your greatest resources as a junior high worker. There have been many occasions when I have looked into the face of a twelve-or thirteen-year-old who was having a problem of one kind or another and recognized myself as a boy around that age. That realization would help tremendously as I listened to him and attempted to relate to him and offer guidance.

If your memory will not cooperate with you on this, it's not likely that you will need to go to a psychiatrist or a hypnotist for therapy. Sometimes just being around junior highers a lot will do the trick. You might talk to people who knew you well when you were a junior higher (like your parents, if possible). Sometimes it's helpful just to try to write down as much as you can remember about those years.

Regardless of whether or not you are able to instantly recall your youth, it is wise to read as many books and articles on adolescent psychology as you can get your hands on. There are many books on the subject in your public library, which have been written by experts who offer many valuable insights into why young people, particularly junior highers, behave the way they do. The chapters in this book dealing with the characteristics of junior highers will hopefully be helpful to you as well, and I have listed other resources for futher reading in the back of this book. Doing some homework of this kind is an excellent way not only to stay informed but also to jolt the memory when remembering does not come easy.

Keep in mind that the reason for all this remembering, reading, and the like is to bring about a better understanding of junior highers and an identification with their problems and feelings. Without this, it becomes very difficult to meet the demands of being a junior high worker. Junior highers often appear to exaggerate their miseries and to overdramatize their suffering, and it's hard to be very supportive when deep down we just don't believe that things are as bad as they let on. And, of course, its entirely possible that they may not be. But to the junior higher, his suffering is very real indeed, and adult advice, criticism, and analysis is the last thing he needs in a moment of crisis. When a person is hurting, he needs a soothing balm; he needs some encouragement, a shoulder to cry on, someone who will listen and understand. When a junior higher tells you that he or she is the ugliest person in his or her peer group, believe it. You have been given an important piece of data. That acceptance must come first; advice, reason and perspective can come later.

Like many kids going through puberty, I had my share of romantic experiences when I was in junior high school. Whenever I would fall in love with the girl who sat on the other side of the classroom, or with the pastor's daughter, or whoever the lucky girl happened to be at the time, I was certain that it was the real thing. Someday we would be married, have kids, live happily ever after, and so on. But the adults in my life, parents especially, would only smile and to my great dismay classify it as puppy love. I can't describe how much pain that caused. In retrospect, I would be willing to admit that it was indeed puppy love of one kind or another, but one thing I have learned over the years, both from experience as a kid and as a youth worker, is that puppy love is very real to puppies.

Learning to Like Them

I recently conducted a survey of over seven hundred junior high kids from all over the United States, and I asked each young person to answer a number of questions. One of the questions was: "If you could ask any question and get a straight answer, what would it be?"

Naturally, I received many different responses, but there was one that appeared over and over again. It seems that the question on the minds of many, if not most, junior highers is simply, "Do you like me?"

They want to know if they are liked and accepted. They aren't overly concerned about the theological issues of the day, or how they can be better Christians at school, or what the future holds. The real issue that gets top priority with so many junior highers today is "Am I O.K.? . . . Do you like me?" This is where the "rubber meets the road" for junior highers.

This response from kids across the country only confirms or reinforces what has already been established. Junior highers desperately crave acceptance from adults as well as from their peers, and more often than not they will pledge absolute loyalty to whoever gives it to them. They like to be liked, which is not all that different from anyone else, but their insecurities in this area give it a much greater significance. Their need to be liked is linked closely with their emerging adulthood and their quest for independence; they are not certain whether or not they are indeed "likable," which they perceive to be an important prerequisite for success in the adult world.

The implications of this for junior high workers should be obvious. A good junior high worker is one who genuinely likes junior high kids. This has to be considered a necessity for anyone hoping for a meaningful and productive ministry with junior highers. Understanding is important, but unless you like to be around them, understanding becomes merely an academic exercise. There are many experts in the field of early adolescence who have never developed a liking for the young people whom they know so much about. But to work with them, one has to really like them.

There are degrees of liking of course. You may be one who likes junior highers a great deal or relatively little (that's O.K.), but the important thing is that what you have comes through for the kids to see. It's not enough to simply announce "I like you" now and then and leave it at that. Words rarely make a good substitute for actions. Junior highers need to see words translated into actions. *Show* them that you really like them whenever you can.

Practically speaking, this means that you should try to develop friendships with kids individually. Learn their names—well. I have discovered the hard way that forgetting a junior highers's name can be extremely destructive to a developing relationship. Find out each one's likes and dislikes, their interests, their concerns. Visit their homes, learn their family situations, and in general show them that you really care about them and like to be with them.

I have found that one of the best ways to show junior highers that you really like them is to do things with them that are not required of you. After all, they know that you are going to be involved with them planning programs and meetings, teaching classes, and so on, even visiting them on occasion, because it's your "job." But when you are willing to give up some of your own free time to be with them, that's different. Only a friend would do that.

Perhaps you could take a few kids on a fishing, camping, or backpacking trip, or invite some of them (even on short notice) to a ball game or movie some evening. Try taking kids shopping with you on a Saturday afternoon, or inviting them to your home during the week, or hosting a slumber party. These are all good ways to let kids know that you enjoy their company.

When I was in junior high school, my family went to a small church that didn't have much of a youth program except for a Sunday night youth meeting just before the evening service. Our pastor's younger brother, Jerry, was given the responsibility of leading those youth group meetings for several years. Today, I can't recall much of what happened at any of those Sunday night meetings of almost twenty years ago. But I remember well that every Saturday Jerry would come around in his car and pick up several of us boys and we would shoot baskets, or go bowling, or head for the beach, or just mess around. As a junior higher, I considered him one of my best friends, even though he was ten years older than I, and I know I would have done almost anything for Jerry. During those years when I was having a great deal of trouble finding acceptance from adults and being treated like a real person, Jerry liked me and was my friend. That was more important than great youth meetings. I am certain today that he played a big role in my development both as a person and as a Christian.

Anytime you can give personal attention to your junior highers, you are going to be letting them know that you are serious when you say that you care about them. Sometimes all it takes is a phone call during the week reminding them of something, thanking them for something, asking a favor of them, or just checking up on how they are doing. I have used the mail in much the same way. Junior highers love to get mail, and a personal note now and then helps tremendously to show kids that you think of them more than on Sundays only.

Keep in mind through all this that if you are an adult, you need to retain your identity and not try to give the impression that you are an overgrown kid. Likewise, junior highers need encouragement to just be themselves and not try to be little adults. Your role should be that of an adult friend who sincerely likes them, cares about them, and tries to understand and help whenever possible.

It goes without saying that liking junior highers is not always something that comes naturally, especially as you grow older, but most of the time it is easier than one might think. It does require a commitment, as most relationships do, and it also requires cultivation and care to help it along. In other words, you may have to work at it.

On the other hand, don't just go through the motions. Sincerity is very important when working with junior highers. They do have the ability to recognize play-acting and to spot the phony. They really don't appreciate a person who is over-relating to them or who takes the approach, "I'm not really an adult, I'm one of you." What is most effective is consistency and genuineness. It doesn't make that much difference what you are or what you do, so long as you are not putting on a show. Sincerity is the key.

Giving Them Enough of Your Time

You may have sensed by now that good junior high ministry could require a sizeable portion of your time. It does take time, after all, to build relationships and pay personal attention to a group of young people, not to mention all the meetings, classes, outings, and the like. Time is a very important factor in the potential effectiveness of a junior high worker in the church, and the time demands can be discouraging. Rarely does anyone have more than enough time to give to an activity. The problem is usually finding any time at all with today's busy schedules.

Speaking from personal experience, this shortage of time can be the downfall of any well-intentioned junior high worker. One may like and understand junior highers very well but just be too busy to put any of it into practice. For this reason, I always list as a prerequisite for the junior high worker, a willingness to allocate enough of his or her time to do an adequate job. The actual amount of time required will vary a great deal from person to person, but it is certain that it will take more than an hour or two on Sunday.

Time plays such an important role because it is tied up with the fact that junior highers view things pretty much in black and white categories. That is, you are either a friend to them or you are not. When you say one thing, and fail to (or are unable to) back it up with your actions, you are often thought of as a hypocrite. That, of course, is not always an accurate assessment of the situation, but proving otherwise can sometimes be a problem. Junior highers characteristically fail to understand adult obligations, and they often take this to mean that some task is more important than they are.

A case in point is a youth sponsor I know who in one month cancelled two meetings scheduled to be held at his home because (1) he needed to work on his car and (2) he wanted to entertain visiting relatives. Of course, it was no suprise that attendance at the following month's meetings dropped considerably.

You don't have to make junior high ministry a full-time job (although it certainly can be), but it is wise to avoid overextending yourself with too many other commitments if you want to do the best job possible. Many times a junior higher worker will run into problems because he or she also works with the senior highs, the college group, directs the choir, moonlights as janitor, and has about fourteen other positions in the church as well. It is also possible for all kinds of nonchurch interests and responsibilities to interfere, and in many cases it is likely that a junior high worker is simply trying to do too much on his own.

Getting Help When It's Needed

Junior high ministry requires a lot from you in the way of time, effort, and creativity, but you really don't have to do it all by yourself. It's easy to become so overwhelmed by the task that you allow discouragement and frustration to settle in, and then nothing is accomplished. Hopefully this book will encourage you to commit yourself enthusiastically to junior high ministry and will also challenge you with some high ideals that call for excellence. Junior high ministry is not an impossible task, but it is a very important one—one that deserves the very best we have to offer. Whenever you feel overwhelmed by it all, that's the time to seek some help.

You may be the kind of person who can do everything yourself, but it is more likely that if you are single-handedly ministering to the junior highers in your church, regardless of the size of the group, you could benefit from some help. If you are a youth director or Christian Education director with a number of age groups to minister to, you are also no doubt in need of other adults who can serve as junior high sponsors, teachers, and the like.

Many times the size of the group will require additional adult leaders. A good ratio is approximately one adult for every eight junior highers. It's difficult to establish relationships with many more than that. It can be done, of course, but it's much more difficult, especially with the many other responsibilities of adult life. If you hope to be able to give some quality time to each person, it is wise not to bite off more than you can chew. As you are probably well aware of, it is possible to have so much to do that you do nothing at all.

Another important consideration is the male-female balance of the group. If you are a male but your group is made up of quite a few girls, you should have a female co-worker who can relate to those girls as only another female can. Junior high girls are just beginning to deal with their emerging womanhood, and they need adult women whom they can trust and confide in. The reverse is also true. It's not being at all sexist to recognize that boys should have men they can relate to and look up to and girls should have women.

A common problem for many young male junior high workers is how to handle thirteen-and fourteen-year-old girls who "fall in love" with them. I don't have an easy answer for that one, but one good way to prevent or rectify situations like this is to work with a woman who can help to minister to the girls in the group.

The problem, of course, is not usually the failure to know when more help is needed. The problem is knowing *who* to enlist. For reasons already stated, there is rarely a waiting list of people who want to work with junior high kids. Usually those who do emerge are what I call "chronic volunteerers"—people who have also volunteered for every other job in the church. To wait for volunteers is not the best way to get qualified workers. It's best to take the initiative yourself and seek out people whom you have reason to believe would make capable junior high workers.

Anyone who works as a teacher, counselor, youth group sponsor, or in a similar capacity with junior highers in the church should be reasonably qualified to do so; that is, they should possess to some degree the qualifications previously stated in this chapter. As a rule of thumb, I usually seek out people who have the time (not too busy), who like (or at least do not dislike) junior highers, and who have not repressed their adolescence so much that they find it impossible to relate to or identify with junior highers. From that point, there is usually room for improvement, Lord willing.

When looking for junior high workers, I have found that it is generally best to rule out high school students. That's not to say that high school youth cannot be quite helpful in a variety of other ways, but they usually lack the maturity necessary to minister with much depth. There are exceptions of course, but they are rare. For two years I directed junior high camps at a large Christian conference center, and invariably those groups with high-school-age cabin counselors were the most difficult. It was not uncommon for us to have to discipline male counselors who had become overly zealous about "counseling" some of the more attractive female campers long after the evening meetings were over. High school students may be fully capable of assisting in many areas, but it is better to seek more mature leadership.

College students often make very good junior high workers, but there are problems common to this age group as well. One is that they may be transient—here this semester, gone the next, or away for the summer. It is best to find people who can give the junior high group a degree of stability over two or three years if possible.

One junior high ministry that I am familiar with asks a three year commitment of its sponsors. Each sponsor (a man, for example) at the beginning of his term is given a group of six to eight seventh grade boys and he works with those boys for three full years through seventh, eighth, and ninth grade) until they move on to the high school department of the church. Of course in practice, this model is no more free from breakdown than any other, but the reasoning is sound. For three years each junior higher in the group has someone who knows him well and really notices whenever he or she is having difficulty or is making progress. The end result of such a plan should be a lower dropout rate as well as a more effective, need-centered ministry.

Parents often want to work with the junior high group, and depending on who the parents are, that can be either good or bad. Some parents feel that they need to spend as much time as they can with their own kids, so they want to work with the junior high group. This is not all bad, but neither is it the best motivation for becoming involved in junior high ministry. Some parents feel that because they have junior highers of their own, that automatically qualifies them as experts and therefore as good junior high workers. Maybe so. Others are concerned that the junior high group is not quite up to par by their standards, and they want to help out, at least for as long as their own kids are in it.

Parents can and should be involved in the junior high program in some way, but again, there are some potential problems with parents doubling as junior high workers. They may be overly protective of their own kids or perhaps too close to them to deal with them in an objective manner. A bigger problem is that their kids are more than likely going to be intimidated by the presence of their parent(s) in the youth group, which prevents them from opening up as they might under normal conditions. Most junior highers are involved, either quietly or overtly, in a struggle to free themselves from parental domination, and they usually need adults other than their parents to relate to during this time.

Having said that, however, I would not rule out parents of junior highers as leaders for the junior high group, especially if they sincerely want to be involved and appear to be qualified to do so. It's strictly a judgment call. I would be very selective if I were in a position to decide, and I would try to help such parents to avoid problems that might arise.

So to whom can you go for help? Who does that leave?

Young adults, either single or married and in their twenties and thirties, make excellent junior high workers. Young couples with no children or with young children often make good husband and wife teams in a junior high group. Older adults whose children have grown, or those of retirement age, are many times quite qualified and may be willing to work with the junior highs in the church. So long as they enjoy the kids and are able to understand and communicate with them, they have all that it takes. Many times kids will love and respect older folks more than those closer to their own age.

One of the most creative junior high workers I have ever met is in his sixties. He teaches a Sunday school class of seventh and eighth grade boys in a small town in the Pacific Northwest. Once a month he has his class wear old clothes to church; instead of attending services that week, they all climb into the back of his camper and go fishing. He provides the boys with bait, tackle, and even shows them how to tie flies. And according to him, he gets more teaching done along the banks of a stream once a month than he is able to accomplish during the three weeks spent in the classroom.

I wouldn't doubt it at all.

Other Places to Go for Help

The important thing to keep in mind is that there are lots of ways to make your job a little easier as a junior high worker. You don't have to do it all by yourself or start from scratch with everything. Get help when it's needed, either by recruiting additional junior high workers to share the load or by making use of other people and resources. Just keep in mind that you will have to go after these things yourself. Help rarely comes calling on its own.

There is an abundance of printed resources that are loaded with ideas to make the programming end of junior high ministry a lot less time-consuming. You don't have to be original with everything you do. I have always maintained that the essence of creativity is the ability to *copy* well what has already been done, and this holds true in youth work too. Many hundreds of hours have gone into developing the resources that are at your disposal, and the more you use other people's ideas, the easier it becomes to create ideas of your own.

There are numerous seminars, workshops, and training events held at various times of the year all over the country, sponsored by denominational groups and by independent organizations and dealing specifically with youth ministry. It is not always convenient to attend those requiring a great deal of travel, time, or expense, but these conferences are excellent ways to get a shot in the arm when you may be needing it most.

In addition, there are undoubtedly junior high workers from other churches in your area who would probably appreciate getting together with you periodically for sharing ideas and support. At times you will find that you are able to pool resources with other churches and possibly schedule some activities together. This is especially beneficial for smaller youth groups.

You may also find it helpful to form a support group of parents and other interested persons in the church who are able to meet with you whenever necessary to discuss some of your concerns, to help with planning, and to pray for the junior high ministry of the church. There are probably a number of people in your congregation who are unable to work with the junior highers week after week but who have much to offer in an advisory or supporting role.

The kids themselves can be a big help to you as well. You don't have to do everything for them. Junior highers are capable of taking on responsibility, and they usually enjoy it. It's a good rule of thumb not to give them more than they can handle or complete within a reasonable length of time, however. They can become easily frustrated or bored with the whole thing if it seems too big. But be on the lookout for ways they can be involved; not only will the kids benefit, but they will also save you a lot of work in the process.

The Junior High Worker as Model

A final note regarding the junior high worker: It is unavoidable that any adult who works with junior highers is putting himself into the role of model. Junior highers are leaving their childhood and are in the process of becoming adults; they are watching closely the adults in their lives to determine what it must be like to be one. This is one of the reasons why it is very important for adults to be adults and not try to be kids. We as adults need to show them what adulthood is really like, and at the same time give them good models for them to pattern their lives.

With this in mind, allow kids to see more than just one side of you as you minister to them. Many times kids will only see the funny, enthusiastic, creative youth worker who seems to have all the answers and never has any problems. That, of course, is in stark contrast to their parents, who always seem to be complaining, grouchy, broke, uptight, and have all kinds of problems. Hopefully you will allow your junior highers to see your whole self.

Notes

[1] Edward Martin, "The Early Adolescent in School," in *Twelve to Sixteen: Early Adolescence*, p. 193.

[2] John A. Rice, *I Came Out of the Eighteenth Century* (New York: Harper & Bros., 1942).

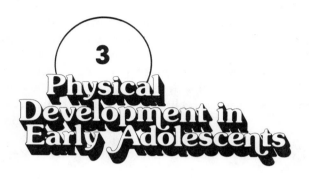

3
Physical Development in Early Adolescents

The next few chapters will deal with the important characteristics of junior highers. There are certain characteristics that make junior highers different from other people, and we'll treat them in five areas: the physical, mental, social, emotional, and spiritual. As we acknowledge the most common characteristics of junior highers, we will also deal with their implications. Our aim will be to relate what is known about junior highers to ministry in the church. It is not enough to merely describe junior high kids. Most people know what one looks and acts like. What we want to do is see how all of this affects the way we work with and relate to junior highers.

It always makes good sense to start with needs when one is attempting to minister to a particular group of people. Need-centered ministry is simply discovering or defining a person's specific needs, and then trying, if possible, to find effective ways to meet those needs. To use a comparision, a doctor will diagnose a patient carefully before administering treatment or before prescribing a cure. Obviously not every patient requires the same kind of treatment. What is good for one may be disastrous for another. Just because something worked for one patient doesn't mean it will be helpful for all. The doctor must begin with each patient's specific needs.

As we examine the characteristics of junior highers, our goal will be to identify their specific needs. From there we can talk about programming. Too often the tendency in the church is to operate in reverse and build around programs rather than around needs. This is no doubt encouraged by all the "It worked for me and it will work for you" books and seminars that offer the very latest in techniques, ideas, strategies, and the like. Program ideas are very helpful, of course (some pretty good ones are included in this book), but that's not the place to start. Every idea or method should be carefully chosen on the basis of the particular needs of the group or of individuals. There are many ideas that work, but not all of them meet needs.

This brings us back to the characteristics of junior high kids. Early adolescents offer us a variety of needs that have to be dealt with if effective ministry is to take place. Junior highers differ significantly from other age groups. A good junior high worker should know what those differences are and then act or program accordingly, in the best interests of the kids.

Unfortunately, there remains a considerable gap between what we know about junior highs and how we treat them. This is true not only in our churches but in the public schools as well. According to Don Wells, principal of the Carolina Friends School:

> When attempting to construct a program for the early adolescent, one is immediately struck by the wide disparity between the data we have on the early adolescent and the programmatic response we devise. . . .
> 1) FACT: Early adolescents need to try on a wide variety of roles. RESPONSE: We class them in . . . a few roles to make them a manageable lot.
> 2) FACT: Early adolescents vary enormously . . . in

physical, mental and emotional maturity and capability. RESPONSE: In schools chronologic age is still the overwhelming factor used in grouping students.

3) FACT: During early adolescence the development of control over one's own life through conscious decision making is crucial. RESPONSE: Adults make all meaningful decisions for almost all early adolescents almost all of the time, but do give the early adolescent the "freedom" to make the "safe" . . . decisions.

4) FACT: Early adolescence is an age where all natural forces (muscular, intellectual, glandular, emotional, etc.) are causing precipitous peaks and troughs in their entire being. RESPONSE: We demand internal consistency of the early adolescent, and in schools even punish some for not achieving this consistent state despite the fact that it is totally impossible for many to achieve at this point in development.

5) FACT: Early adolescents need space and experience to "be" different persons at different times. RESPONSE: We expect them to "be" what they said they were last week because otherwise we cannot [use forethought in dealing with them].

6) FACT: Early adolescents are preoccupied by physical and sexual concerns, frightened by their perceived inadequacy. RESPONSE: We operate with them each day not as though this were a minor matter in their lives, but as though such concerns did not exist at all.

7) FACT: Early adolescents need a distinct feeling of present importance, a present relevancy of their own lives now. RESPONSE: We place them in institutions called "junior high schools" which out of hand stress their subordinate status to their next maturational stage, and then feed them a diet of watered down "real stuff."[1]

In the next five chapters we will focus on many of the characteristics of early adolescents that have relevance for junior high workers in the church and that demand our attention. Keep in mind that I do not intend to duplicate or replace any of the outstanding writing on early adolescence by leading doctors, psychologists, educators, and researchers. All of these people are more qualified than I to give the subject a more scholarly and thorough treatment. In fact, I cannot overemphasize to you the importance of reading as much as you can about this age group from other sources, particularly the work of Erik Erikson, Peter Blos, J. M. Tanner, Jean Piaget, and Lawrence Kohlberg. Although we will only be scratching the surface, we will try to cover in as much depth as necessary those areas of special significance to the junior high worker in the church.

Keep in mind also that we will be making a lot of *generalizations*, which is often a very dangerous thing to do when you are talking about people. After hearing me talk about junior highers, a number of youth workers have told me that I was "way off base," because one or more kids in their junior high group didn't fit my description of the "typical" early adolescent. In all probability, they were absolutely correct (about the kids in their group, that is). Everyone is different from everyone else, and it is wise to avoid putting people into little boxes. No two people are exactly alike.

This is one of the reasons it is important that you do not look at your junior high group as a "group." Instead, you must see them as John, Tim, Mary Lou, Peggy, Don, Mike, and so on. Your group is a collection of persons who are all different and who have different needs at different times. That's one of the challenging and exciting things about ministry in the church, and it is especially true with junior highers.

Nevertheless, there are some things that can be said about junior high kids in general that are accurate *in most cases*. That's about the best anyone can do. Some kids are way ahead of schedule, some are far behind, and others seem to skip certain stages altogether. It's part of your job to get to know each person individually. There will be exceptions. In the meantime, we must do the best we can with generalities. To not do so, only because there are going to be some exceptions, is foolish. Our generalities are based on the observations of experts as well as those of hundreds of experienced junior high workers, and from my own years of involvment with kids.

From Children into Adults: Puberty Strikes

> Puberty, next to birth itself, is the most drastic change we experience in life, but unlike birth, we are acutely aware of the exciting transitions through which we pass. . . .[2]

Probably the most important physical characteristic of junior highers is that they are going through puberty. Their bodies are going through an enormous change. It only happens once in a person's lifetime; the child is transformed into an adult. Physically, both boys and girls develop into men and women mostly while they are in junior high school.

The average age for menarche, when a girl has her first menstrual period, is 12.9 years. The female adolescent growth spurt actually begins much earlier, at around 9.6 years. Its peak velocity is at about age 11.8. Comparable milestones occur almost two years later for boys.[3] This is why girls are usually bigger than boys during early adolescence and are more fully developed. The boys don't catch up with the girls physically until around age fifteen or so. Sometimes junior high boys become a little frustrated when their girl friends become interested in older boys.

While the above figures are fairly accurate, they cannot be viewed as absolutes. You may have two boys, for instance, who are the same age, but who are two years apart in physical development. This is quite normal.

It is a fact that the average age for the onset of puberty has been dropping steadily for decades. Sixty years ago in America the average age of menarche was 14.3 years compared to today's 12.9.[4] In other countries, the downward trend has been even more severe as they become more "civilized." Coinciding with this earlier maturation has been an increase in height and weight. Most of the experts have concluded that this has been caused primarily by better nutrition, particularly more protein and calories at infancy. Because people are bigger, they experience puberty earlier. Height and weight seem to be the dominant factors.

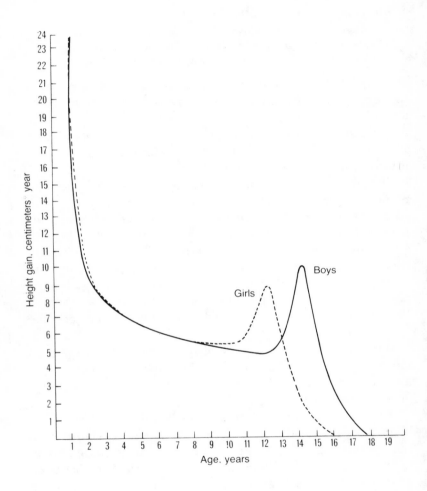

Typical velocity curves for length or height in boys and girls. These curves represent the velocity of the typical boy or girl at a given instant. From J. M. Tanner, R. H. Whitehouse, and M. Takaishi, "Standards from Birth to Maturity for Height, Weight Height Velocity and Weight Velocity; British Children, 1965," *Archives of Disease in Childhood* 41 (1966); 455-71. (*A centimeter equals .39 inch.)

It seems unlikely that this trend will continue, however, or we could have kids going through puberty before entering kindergarten in the not too distant future. While some researchers hold that the trend toward an earlier onset of puberty is going on unabated, at least one study, by the National Center for Health Statistics, claims that there has been no significant change in the last twenty years and that the trend has already leveled off.[5]

Regardless of the age, the bottom line is that children are in the process of becoming adults. It is unfortunate that in our culture, this fact is hardly acknowledged, but in many ancient cultures (and in some cultures today) as soon as a boy or girl manifests the physical signs of adulthood (menarche, breasts, pubic hair, size, etc.), they take on adult roles immediately.

There are definite rites, or ceremonies, to make the passage from childhood to adulthood quick, clear, and sure. Before these rites, one is a child; after the rites, one is accepted into the company of women and men. For girls these rites have included such events as the celebration of the arrival of the first menstruation, formal training in the skills of providing sexual satisfaction to one's husband, and wearing new apparel or other symbols of maturity.

With boys, who do not experience a spectacular, defined, and observable event such as menarche, there comes a time when the young male would be taken off in the company of men, perhaps circumcised, tutored in the duties and privileges of mangood, and allowed to emerge a man. Among American Indians, the boy goes out alone on a "vision quest." He finds a spiritual helper and returns, reborn, with a new name, his name as a man. There is no doubt when the passage is completed. It is more like the canoeist crossing a river than negotiating a run of white water.[6]

In our culture, this passage is not nearly so clear-cut or brief. We ask emerging adults to wait another six or seven years before claiming adulthood. This is no doubt a reason for much of the sexual temptation and frustration faced by modern teens. They have to put it on hold. They are required to contain or muzzle these natural urges and today many are unwilling to do this.

It might be interesting to note here that the trend toward an earlier onset of puberty in recent decades, combined with modern culture's trend toward later marriages, more education, and the like, has created a special group of people that many cultures never had to deal with before: teen-agers. In fact, the term "teen-ager" was not really a part of the English language until the 1940s and it was not until then (or later) that youth work began to emerge as a necessity, let alone a specialty. With this in mind, we can understand why there hasn't been more progress in the field of youth work. Perhaps youth work itself is still in its infancy, with much yet to learn. Welcome to the frontier.

A New Awareness of the Body

With the onset of puberty comes a newly acquired awareness of the body. Junior highers are commonly concerned about how they look—whether or not they are good-looking or attractive and how they measure up to others their own age. They are, in their own secret fears, growing too rapidly, too slowly, too unevenly, too tall, or developing too much in the wrong places. And for many, these fears are justified. Physical growth can be very uneven and unpredictable during early adolescence, and this can be the source of much anxiety and grief.

Most junior highers worry a great deal about how they are going to turn out. They know that someday they are going to stop growing, and there's nothing that can be done about it then. So they worry about it now. It's not an overt thing with most kids, however. You won't find them walking down the street fretting aloud about how they are developing physically. It is a hidden fear; often it affects their lives in ways they are not even aware of at the time. The slow developer, for example, may for reasons he cannot even understand feel out of place or afraid and compensate by becoming either withdrawn or boisterous.

The junior higher's social life is affected dramatically by this physical development. To illustrate this, consider my five-year-old son. He will play and become best of friends with any other child, regardless of size, color, looks, sex, or whatever. I never cease to be amazed at how little children can become instant friends with almost anyone, anytime, with hardly any limitations. But as children grow older, and this usually coincides with the beginning of puberty, this innocence fades. Kids become much more selective in their associations. Suddenly there emerges a popular group and an unpopular group. Popular kids don't have much to do with unpopular kids, and unpopular kids rarely associate with popular kids. It's an extremely rigid class system that lasts for quite a few years, and it is particularly noticeable during the junior high years. It's a terrible thing in the eyes of most kids to be unpopular, and of course, it's everyone's dream to be among the popular elite. When you are in this select group, acceptance by others, positions of leadership, and a life "happily ever after" is virtually assured.

What is it that makes a person popular or unpopular? Ninety-nine times out of a hundred it will have something to do with physical characteristics such as how you look or how well developed you are. Boys who are athletic, tall, and handsome tend to be popular. Girls who are pretty, with attractive figures, nice hair, and so on are likely to be popular. If you are ugly (or merely plain), short, fat, or skinny, you may be doomed to be an undistinguished member of the "out" crowd, a fate worse than death. For this reason, junior highers place a great deal of emphasis on physical characteristics. They must. It's almost a matter of survival.

A junior high girl may become preoccupied with her appearance, because she may have the idea that her entire future is dependent on it. She may think that if she isn't pretty, she may face not only being unpopular, but also she won't have dates, she won't get married, she won't be able to get a job or have kids, and so on. This world view, distorted as it may be, leaves some girls in a state of depression and despair. Others will embark on a strenuous program to repair whatever "defects" they may have with cosmetics, exercises, diets, and an endless quest for that miracle product that will make them look like Miss Cover Girl.

This need is reflected in early adolescent ideals as well. In the surveys I have taken of junior highers, nearly all list as their heroes the most glamorous people in show business or in sports. Their favorite television programs are those featuring heroic, beautiful, athletic, almost superhuman characters who are always successful and, most importantly, well liked and admired by all. In response to the question, "If you could change anything about yourself, what would it be?" the answers invariably had to do with a physical improvement—a new nose, new hair, new face, new shape, or a whole new body. This dissatisfaction with themselves, by the way, causes some to have a deep resentment toward God, for He created them in the first place. When this is the case, it may need to be dealt with before the junior higher will show much interest in or enthusiasm for spiritual things.

On the other hand, the message of the gospel can be very appealing to junior highers at this very point. They may feel inadequate or inferior because of their failure to measure up to the world's criteria for beauty or success, but Christ offers hope in the midst of all that. No one is plain or ordinary in the kingdom of God. We are all created in His image, which makes each of us a reflection of the very essence of God. We are special, despite the world's standards, because God loves us.

We must be careful as junior high workers not to contradict the very gospel we teach. We should instead reinforce it by the way we relate to junior highers individually, and also by our choice of programming. For example, it's going to be difficult to convince a junior higher that God really doesn't care whether or not he or she is glamorous or athletic when all we offer them is glamorous Christian celebrities (former beauty queens, famous football heroes, ex-rock stars, etc.) as models. If we do this, kids will be sufficiently impressed and may engage in some harmless or even healthy "Christian" hero worship, but they may also rule out the possibility that God can use them just as he used the famous celebrity, especially if they are feeling rather inadequate in the first place.

What's Happening to Them

The junior higher's body changes in many ways during puberty, and these changes are accompanied by an equal number of puzzling new experiences—some exciting, some embarrassing, and others just plain awful. When they occur, it's hard for many early adolescents to understand them or adjust to them. What makes it even worse is that no one talks much about them either, and those who do are often misinformed.

For girls, one of the most noticeable of these changes is a general acceleration in both height and weight, a widening of the hips, and the appearance of breasts. At this age, girls become softer, rounder, and grow very concerned about their figure. They want very much to look good in a two-piece bathing suit at the beach or pool, and they hope they will be attractive to members of the opposite sex.

This can be a very frustrating time for girls who are convinced that they are growing too much or too little in the wrong places and who insist upon comparing themselves to others or to girls they see in fashion magazines. Breasts, especially, have become such a preoccupation in our society, becoming almost synonymous with sex appeal, that it is not surprising that girls with small breasts often fear that boys will never like them. Girls become anxious, too, if one breast grows faster than the other (as they sometimes do) or if their breasts are growing too large too soon. A girl with "too much" is often the object of considerable ridicule from other girls and some rather unpleasant joking from the boys. Most girls could benefit from some assurance at this point that sex appeal is rarely dependent on the breasts or any other part of the anatomy for that matter. Breasts, like women, come in all shapes and sizes.

During junior high school girls also experience their first period, which can be a real shock if they aren't prepared for it. Accidents occur at the worst times and are very embarassing. Again, girls often worry that there is something wrong with them. Menstruation for junior high girls is just like it is for older women in that it is frequently accompanied by abdominal pains, lack of energy, and ocasional irritability. Also, it takes a while before most junior high girls have their period on a regular twenty-eight-day cycle. They might go three months without having a period, and then have two very close together, and so on. Hopefully, someone is able to assure them that all this is normal.

For boys, the big frustration during junior high school is that they don't develop as early as the girls do, which creates a rather awkward situation for them when it comes to relating to these girls. They may still be trying to impress them with their skateboards and Yo-Yo's while the girls are becoming more impressed with boys who have a driver's license.

When boys do experience the onset of puberty, they grow at a rapid and uneven pace. It is not uncommon for boys to grow as much as six inches in one year, yet the arms, legs, and trunk may grow disproportionately, resulting in awkwardness and clumsiness. Just when a boy is becoming more coordinated, puberty strikes and his forward progress may be impaired or set back. Appetites increase dramatically at this age as well. Most junior high boys can easily outeat adults. The voice usually changes too, which provides some embarassing moments for members of the junior high boys' choir.

Another telltale sign of approaching manhood is the emergence of pubic hair. For boys, pubic hair is similar in significance to breasts for girls. Until you grow a crop of pubic hair around the genitals, your manhood remains in doubt. Taking a shower after a P. E. class can be a traumatic experience for a slow developer. As a junior high camp director, I have noticed boys who had hardly changed their underwear the entire week of camp for fear of being ridiculed. In addition, boys are encountering new sexual urges and feelings during puberty and this can be a source of needless worry and guilt. Wet dreams, masturbation, and erections (at the most awkward times) are common signs of a developing sexuality. Junior high boys become extremely curious about the opposite sex and about sex in general, and they usually manage to get their hands on magazines like *Playboy* or *Penthouse* to satisfy that curiosity.

Helping Them to Understand It All

When I was in junior high school I automatically assumed that my sexuality was sinful or at least undesirable simply because it was "unmentionable." No one ever talked about sex at church, and I for one was afraid to ask. Since my parents were Christians, I figured they probably wouldn't want to talk about it either.

Things haven't really changed that much in twenty years, although the public schools have picked up much of the slack in sex education in recent years. I recently asked junior highers in a survey, "Where do you get your information about sex?" Most answered "School," but it is hard to know whether this is from health education classes or from friends. The second and third most common answers were "friends" and "parents." Other typical answers were: "TV," "Books," "Porno magazines," "Movies," "Myself," "By doing it," "On the streets," "I keep my ears open," "Wherever I can get it," "Nowhere," "Nobody gives me a straight answer." One girl replied, "I refuse to answer that question because it doesn't belong in church." It is revealing that although all seven hundred junior highers surveyed were members of church youth groups, only three kids indicated that they had received any information about sex from their church or church youth leaders.

Even in our present "age of enlightenment," there are many

early adolescents who remain uninformed and ignorant concerning their sexuality and how their bodies are changing. Last year, for example, my wife and I took in a foster child only one week old, whose mother, we found out later, was fourteen years old. Incredible as it sounds, she did not even know she was pregnant until she went to the doctor with severe "pains." It was only a few hours later that she gave birth to a six-pound baby girl.

I am not suggesting that the church must conduct sex-education classes during Sunday school, but it would seem appropriate for youth workers, particularly junior high workers, to let kids know that they can feel free to talk about it in church. After all, God created sex in the first place, and it's unlikely He would be embarrassed by having it discussed in His house. Junior highers should be able to get straight answers to their questions from a Christian point of view. They are already getting answers from every other point of view.

Of course, some people (especially parents) think that if they don't bring up the subject, then kids won't be concerned about it. They argue that talking about sex will only make kids more curious or overstimulate them and encourage experimentation. Unfortunately it just doesn't work that way. Ignoring the subject doesn't make it go away. Sooner or later (usually sooner) there comes a time when kids must have the information and guidance they need concerning their bodies, and if they don't get it at home or at church or at school, they'll get it somewhere else.

If we really believe in need-centered ministry, then it would seem only natural to consider the junior highers' need to know about the changes that are taking place in their bodies. They need assurance that what is happening is good. God is not trying to make life miserable for junior high kids. They need to know that these changes are normal, not something to be ashamed of or afraid of. Puberty happened to all of us, and despite that, we came through it pretty well. So will they.

Confusing the Physical With the Spiritual

The junior high years can be a time of real spiritual letdown for many kids who construe their physical problems to be spiritual ones. An early adolescent boy, for example, may feel that he is not much of a Christian because he is lazy and hates to do chores, homework, clean up his bedroom, or work hard in the youth program at church. He lacks the necessary motivation, finds it hard to follow through on anything he starts, and feels sure that somehow he must have lost his faith somewhere along the way. What he probably doesn't realize is that in reality he is a normal junior higher going through a normal part of growing up. Anyone who grows several inches in less than a year is going to be fatigued. The solution is not necessarily to make another commitment to Christ. It is more likely that the answer is simply to get plenty of rest and to do the best you can under the circumstances.

Junior highers may have similar guilt feelings regarding their sexuality. Boys may feel certain that they are committing unpardonable sins when they have wet dreams, masturbate, or get "turned on" by an attractive girl. Again, if any of these things do reach problem proportions, the answer is not to call an emergency prayer meeting. Perhaps a cold shower is in order. These things happen to junior highers because they are junior highers, not because they are backslidden Christians.

Avoid Embarrassing Them Needlessly

Junior highers can be very cruel at times, taking every opportunity to point out deficiencies in each other whenever it is to their advantage. They think that by making fun of someone else, they are making themselves look superior. Usually junior highers are able to bounce back without any problem after some good-natured ribbing, but ridicule and the accompanying embarrassment can be very damaging to relationships and to self-esteem. It is important, therefore, that we avoid as much as possible situations in which kids might be looked

down on because of ability, handicap, appearance, or physical
development in general.

As a junior higher, I was a slow developer and not as athletic
as other boys my age. Because of that, I loathed P. E. classes at
school. I enjoyed playing games and competition as much as
anyone, but I still dreaded it when it came time to choose up
teams (nearly an everyday occurrence). I was inevitably chosen
last, and this was humiliating every time. I don't blame anyone
for not choosing me first, but it was humiliating all the same.

Actually, the games and activities themselves were often the
biggest reason I was not particularly fond of P. E. We played
football (I always got to block, never play quarterback. I rarely
ever touched the ball!) and other seasonal sports—softball,
basketball, and, worst of all, track. I probably still hold the
record at Pleasant Valley School for the slowest 50-yard dash
ever run by a seventh grader, and I ran it in plain view of all my
classmates. We would also see who could do the most chin-ups,
push-ups, and so on, and it was there in P. E. that my status as a
loser became firmly established for the next few years.

I have included in this book some great games for junior
highers that I wish I could have played when I was in junior
high school. They were chosen because they are not only fun to
play, but they can also be played by practically anyone, regardless of ability. With these games, everyone has an equal chance
to win, because the game either requires no skill or it requires
skills that no one has ever heard of. Competition is fine for
junior highers, but competition should never drive a wedge
between the skilled and the unskilled, the "good" and the
"bad."

Despite all that you or anyone else can do, there is no way to
prevent junior highers from experiencing some embarrassment as long as they are around other people. It's normal and
inevitable. But a good junior high worker will at least be
sensitive in this area and try to find ways to help each person to
feel accepted, liked, and an important part of the group.

Help Them to Find Affirmation in Other Areas

When I was in ninth grade, I was arrested for shoplifting. My best friend and I were caught trying to walk out of a store with our coats lined with merchandise, and this ended my rather brief career as a big-time crook. Like most shoplifters, we never needed anything we took. In fact, we usually gave most of it to our friends at school. It was just an exciting game, a challenge, and in retrospect, it was mostly a way for us to prove our manhood, both to ourselves and to others. We hadn't been able to prove it any other way. We had tried out for the freshman football and baseball teams and were unsuccessful. With a couple of badly damaged egos, we needed some way to show that we were, in fact, courageous, brave, tough, independent he-men, and for a while anyway, stealing from local merchants was as good a way as any.

This kind of thinking is not uncommon with early adolescents who are slow developers or who have deep feelings of inferiority. The drive to be accepted by one's peers is a very strong one, and it may cause junior highers to try to compensate for their lack of physical prowess in undesirable or destructive ways. Smoking, drinking, drugs, sex, rowdy behavior, foul language, fighting, joining gangs, running away from home, and breaking the law are only a few manifestations of this.

On the other hand, it is possible for kids to achieve the same thing (peer acceptance, ego-satisfaction, and the like) through positive and constructive means as well. Following my life of crime in ninth grade, I became very interested in art—drawing cartoons, designing posters, and painting signs. Soon this became my "thing." Everyone would come to me for art work, and gradually those feelings of inferiority diminished. I felt proud that the most popular kids in the school would ask me to help with their publicity for school activities or for their student body election campaigns.

Early adolescents need ways to gain a positive identity and a feeling of self-worth, and an important part of a junior high worker's ministry can be to help kids find ways to accomplish this. Art, music, writing, program planning, public speaking, dramatics, leadership, teaching, sports, humor, or just plain helping out are all possibilities. Slow developers, especially, should be given opportunities whenever possible to affirm themselves in areas in which they can excel. Build on their assets and help them feel good about themselves even though they may not be winning the battle on the physical front.

Divide the Group by Age and by Sex

The radical physical changes that take place during early adolescence happen over a very short period of time. A seventh grader is leaving childhood while the ninth grader is on the brink of adulthood, and the differences between them in maturity and capabilities are enormous. There may be more difference between a seventh grade boy and a ninth grade girl than there is between the same ninth grade girl and someone ten years older. This naturally tends to complicate things when trying to find ways to meet the needs of junior highers on both ends of the puberty spectrum and those in between as well.

Until someone comes up with a better way, it would appear that the easiest and best way to maximize the effectiveness of teaching/learning situations is to divide large groups of junior highers by age (or by year in school) and by sex. In other words, in a three-year junior high program, you would have six classes: seventh grade boys, seventh grade girls, eighth grade boys, eighth grade girls, ninth grade boys, and ninth grade girls.

This model may not be possible for small junior high groups, of course, but where I have seen it used, the results have been good. Junior highers are much more willing to open up and enter into discussion with people close to their own age and gender. And with fewer distractions, discipline problems are often reduced considerably. Normally, when trying to teach a large mixed group of seventh, eighth, and ninth graders, there can be difficulty maintaining order simply because the younger ones are trying to show off in front of the older ones, the older ones are irritated by the mere presence of the younger ones, and everyone seems to be threatened or embarrassed by someone else. Communication becomes very difficult. But in smaller, segregated groups, communication is much easier.

It is not necessary to divide the group for all meetings and activities, however. Junior highers need to feel they are part of a larger group; this gives them a sense of belonging and group togetherness. But for classes, discussion groups, and other learning situations, it is usually wise to divide the group up into smaller, more manageable units.

Teaching Them to Take Care of Their Bodies

As junior highers become more aware of their bodies and more concerned about their appearance and physical development, it would be appropriate for youth workers in the church to show kids how proper nutrition and health care can be a reflection of their Christian commitment. Traditionally, churches have shown a great deal of concern for peoples' souls but have not offered much help for their bodies. Since God gave us our bodies, creating each one in His own image, and since they are in fact a "temple of the Holy Spirit" (1 Cor. 6:19) and we are asked to "present our bodies" back to Him (Rom. 12:1), it would be quite consistent with Scripture to help young people to care for their bodies properly.

This is of particular importance when it comes to what the early adolescent eats. Junior highers are true "junk food junkies," and nutritionists are deeply concerned about the long-range effects of today's poor eating habits. The Maternal and Child Health Service reports that the three groups most vulnerable to poor nutrition are infants and young children, adolescents, and expectant mothers. Another nutrition survey indicated that young people between the ages of ten and sixteen had the highest rates of unsatisfactory nutritional status, and boys more than girls. Problems included being underweight or undersize, obesity, iron-deficiency anemia, and dental caries. It is generally agreed that nutrition hits one of its low points during early adolescence. [7]

This is especially bad news when you consider that the adolescent growth spurt is second only to infant growth. The body is developing rapidly, including the brain, which is perhaps the most vulnerable to abuse. There is strong evidence that early malnutrition (in infants) directly affects intellectual competence, but little is known about how nutritional deficiencies affect the brain during later childhood and adolescence. It would seem a logical conclusion, however, that to encourage good eating habits would be of critical importance at this age. You could be doing junior highers in your group a great service by raising their consciousness on this and other health issues.

Notes

[1]From an unpublished manuscript by Donald A. Wells. Used by permission.

[2]Gilman D. Grave, *The Control of the Onset of Puberty* (New York: John Wiley & Sons, 1974), p. xxiii.

[3]Ibid, p. 409.

[4]J. M. Tanner, "Sequence, Tempo, and Individual Variation," in *Twelve to Sixteen, Early Adolescence*, p. 22.

[5]*Youth Report* (Grafton Publications, New York, August 1976), p. 4.

[6]Eric W. Johnson, *How to Live Through Junior High School* (Philadelphia and New York: J. B. Lippincott Co., 1975), p. 39.

[7]Joan Lipsitz, *Growing Up Forgotten* (Lexington, Mass: Lexington Books, 1977), p. 17.

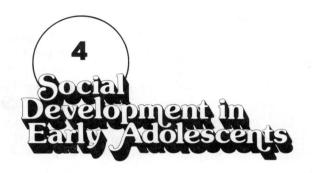

4
Social Development in Early Adolescents

With early adolescence comes a marked increase in social awareness and social maturity that parallels the many physical changes taking place. Peer relationships become very important to junior highers. Prior to this age, they only needed playmates, but now they need and seek out more meaningful friendships. Friends are the very lifeblood of adolescence; they are people who can be trusted, who listen and who understand feelings.[1] Loneliness becomes a new experience for junior highers, and the fear of rejection becomes a source of anxiety and often dictates behavior patterns and value choices. Junior highers will usually do whatever is most conducive to making friends and keeping them.

In my surveys on junior highers, I learned that most junior high students like school, but for one reason: School is first and foremost a place to be with friends. The reverse is also true. Those who strongly dislike school do so usually because their friends are not there or because "enemies" are present there. Teachers, curriculum, facilities, and the like play only a secondary role. The implications of this should be obvious for junior high workers in the church. Youth groups should probably have a good amount of "redeeming social value" in order for junior highers to really enjoy being a part of them.

The Drive for Independence

To understand what is actually happening with junior highers in the social realm, we must begin with another stock theme of adolescent psychology. (By "stock theme," I mean that this is something you can find in practically every book on adolescent behavior, and this leads us to believe that it is common knowledge among experts in the field.) Simply stated, we can say that it is a primary task of early adolescence to break ties with the family and to attempt to establish an identity that is separate from parents or other authority figures.

Junior highers are possessed with a drive toward independence. They want to come up with an identity of their own, to be their own person, and to make their own choices and commitments. The values of their parents won't do any longer. They want to be set free and to be treated like adults. This is the age when kids become highly critical of their parents and consider them to be hopelessly old-fashioned. They may be embarrassed by their parents and prefer not to sit with them in church. While there are certainly exceptions, this behavior is definitely the norm for early adolescents.

This naturally accounts for many of the problems between parents and their early adolescent children. Many parents are caught completely off guard by this. They find it hard to understand why they are suddenly "losing control"; they never had such problems before. Just when their children are finally learning to be good, obedient boys and girls, they become junior highers and appear to take a giant step backward. But it is always wise to remember that adolescent development progresses via the detour of regression, and parents who understand this will find parenting junior highers a much less traumatic experience (although it is never easy).

Many parents may have an understanding of what is going on but are reluctant to allow it to happen. As their children move toward independence, they become more rigid and refuse to let out any rope. This results in clashes and strained parent-child relationships. Parents often need extra help understanding that their young adolescent child is not viciously turning against them. They need to know that the child is more likely trying to discover and establish his own identity as an independent entity and needs to be given opportunities to do so without undue interference. This does not mean, on the other hand, that parents should take an "I don't care" approach; this would be even more disastrous. They should simply work *with* their children rather than against them while they are trying to grow up.

Since I have not yet had the opportunity to be the parent of a junior higher, I will refrain from giving too many "do's and don'ts" for parents. As you can imagine, it is one thing to be a junior high worker and it is another thing altogether to be the parent of a junior higher. Perhaps in ten years or so I will be able to add a few paragraphs to this book under the heading "How I Blew It As a Parent."

The Bridge Toward Independence: The Peer Group

While it is true that the primary goal for the early adolescent is independence, it is also true that it is an impossible goal, at least for the time being. Junior highers do want to be independent, but the gap between the security of the home or parents and this sought-after independence is far too great. To charge out into the world on one's own is a pretty scary thing. Junior highers want to be treated like adults and to think for themselves, but they lack the confidence necessary to take on the responsibilities that go with it. There needs to be a middle ground—something to prepare them for independence.

This is the function of the peer group. The stepping stone or bridge that links dependence with independence is conformity to the peer group. It is ironic that for a junior higher to find his

identity as an individual, he must lose his identity as he becomes part of the crowd. What the crowd does, he does. What
the crowd likes, he likes. It seems just the opposite of independent thinking; a movement away from independence. This
accounts for the many fads so characteristic of the junior high
years as well as the inevitability of cliques and associations that
often seem so destructive. But this conformity, strange as it
may seem, is an essential part of adolescent development and is
very helpful as a way for junior highers to gain the security and
confidence needed for adulthood.

This is described by Howard and Stoumbis:

> In his desire for independence, the early adolescent
> appears to become a rigid conformist to the mores, dress,
> speech, and attitudes of his fellows. Security is found in
> identifying with the group insofar as is at all possible. If
> group standards denigrate strong academic performance,
> then high grades are for "squares" and "goody-goodies."
> The seventh-grade pupil who was a strong student be-
> comes only an average ninth-grade student, which con-
> fuses and shocks his parents and teachers. The early
> adolescent is almost certain to develop an air, a manner of
> sophistication or pseudosophistication, which he hopes
> will cover up the worries, doubts, and feelings of uncer-
> tainty which are usually with him. During this time the
> early adolescent is highly susceptible to undesirable
> influences and individuals—if they are admired by his
> peer group. To gain status and recognition he must con-
> form to these new standards. The role of the school should
> be obvious in developing desirable values, attitudes, and
> standards, and in providing socially approved experi-
> ences and situations.[2]

By conforming to the peer group, the junior higher is subconsciously trying to find out whether or not he is liked and
accepted as a person away from the home. It is only natural that
parents offer acceptance, love, admiration, encouragement,
and security to their children, but now something more is
needed. The early adolescent wants to know if he is equally
O.K. "out there" in the real world. Once he is accepted and

feels secure as part of the group, then he is likely to have enough confidence to step out and to experiment with being "different"—the discovery of his own identity. The peer group becomes in fact the bridge to independence.

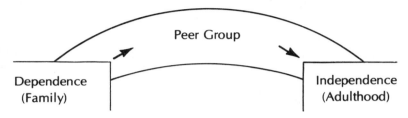

Drawing from personal experience once again, I was very much like my parents, as most youngsters are, during my preteen years. My values, beliefs, and tastes were almost identical to those of my parents. I remember as a child listening to country and western music (and liking it!) because my father did. I knew all the words to "Your Cheatin' Heart" as a fourth grader, and I never missed the "Grand Ole Opry" television show on Saturday nights.

But along about the sixth grade, I discovered that other kids my age did not listen to country music, but to rock-and-roll. And so, much to my parents' dismay, through junior high and most of high school I was a rock-and-roll addict. Country music was for "ignorant hillbillies" (parents included), and there was no way I was going to be caught dead listening to it again. My father and I would fight for control of the radio whenever we got into the car. All the other kids liked rock music, and so did I. It was very important to like the same things my friends liked. To be different was to be foolish.

But as I recall, it was as a senior in high school and during college that I finally dared to leave the security of the crowd. By that time I had courage enough to strike out on my own and be a little different. I became a great fan of folk music and then bluegrass (hillbilly) music. For my parents it was like the return of the Prodigal Son.

That's the way it usually goes with early adolescence. The pattern is predictable enough to say that it is normal and necessary for junior highers to lose their identities in order to find them. Failure to conform (even when the group is doing something wrong) can produce feelings of guilt and inadequacy as severe as the feelings involved in going against one's conscience. Caught between a rock and a hard place, so to speak, the result is often a difficult struggle for the junior higher. He or she knows that either of the choices will lead to painful consequences.

The important thing for adults, particularly for parents, to understand is that this conformity is not all bad. It is true that junior highers are very susceptible during this time; they can choose the wrong kinds of friends and get involved in things we do not approve of, but the alternatives are usually worse. Better a little bad influence than no friends at all. There are a great many adults who are seriously maladjusted emotionally or psychologically simply because they were never able to fit in as adolescents. It is not uncommon to find adults still conforming to every whim of the crowd, hoping to find the acceptance they never received during their youth.

It is hardly ever helpful to junior highers for parents or youth workers to overreact to what must be considered an important part of adolescent development. In the church, it is not uncommon to use Scripture verses such as "Be ye not conformed . . ." as a way of telling kids that they should not be like other kids or that they should only have "approved" friends. It is not likely that Romans 12:2 was intended to be interpreted or used in that way. It seems clear enough that this process of socialization was as much designed by God as puberty itself. It serves a very useful purpose. In the words of educator Jerome Kagan:

> The early adolescent . . . needs many peers to help him sculpt his beliefs, verify his new conclusions, test his new attitudes against an alien set in order to evaluate their hardiness and obtain support for his new set of fragile assumptions.[3]

Allow Them to Choose Their Own Peer Group Commitments

One of the great fears parents have is that their young adolescent children will become part of the "wrong crowd." And usually their fears are justified. It is very easy for junior highers to choose friends who do not hold Christian values and who may exert a negative influence on them. Young people who smoke, drink, use drugs, and worse are often the majority on many junior high school campuses. It is natural to want to protect our children from this kind of behavior, if possible, and to encourage them to choose the right kinds of friends.

But we cannot choose their friends for them. They must have the freedom to make their own choices. We can and should offer guidance, but it is usually destructive in the long run to criticize or to put down the friends that our junior highers select. To do so is to attack their judgment and to show little or no faith in them. When it is apparent that there are some dangers inherent in a particular relationship, then it should certainly be discussed. Antisocial behavior is not necessarily contagious. Psychologist Eda Le Shan states:

> There are times when it is a necessary part of growing up to live through a particular relationship. Much growth and learning about oneself can take place, even in some of the most ill-advised friendships.
> The only real protection against poor friendship choices is whatever help we can give our children in respecting themselves so much that they are unlikely to choose relationships that will hurt or demean them, and that we help them to understand enough about human motivation and behavior to judge others with insight. . . . Surely if a youngster seems to be making one bad choice after another, we might conclude that his perception of his value as a human being is very poor indeed, and under such circumstances we and our child need to seek help in taking a look at this pattern.[4]

Also, as young adolescents most of us made some poor choices of friends, and we pulled through. Chances are pretty good that today's kids will also survive somehow.

Not Ready to Sacrifice Friends for Faith

Junior high ministry can be very rewarding; early adolescents who are trying to think for themselves and make meaningful commitments on their own are often very open and responsive to the message of the gospel. Unlike older teens and adults, junior highers have not become rigid, skeptical, or hardened toward spiritual things. This makes them very reachable without manipulation or coercion being necessary. I have seen hundreds of junior highers choose freely to follow Christ.

But junior highers, young Christians that they are, are rarely able to put much of their faith into practice right away, especially if it means putting their friendships in jeopardy. They are not ready to sacrifice their friends for their faith. As was stated earlier, friends are the very lifeblood of adolescence, and they are crucial to normal adolescent development. If a choice must be made between friends and faith, they will choose their friends nearly every time. Faith can come later. ("When I'm an adult. Then it will be easy.") Having friends is the most important thing now.

What this means for the junior high worker is that it is rather foolish to force kids to choose between friends and faith if it can be avoided. Many times we do this without even realizing it. For example, when we ask them to make certain kinds of public stands (like witnessing, wearing Jesus buttons on their clothes), we are indirectly asking them to make a decision. The junior higher tends to think: *If I do it, the kids will think I'm some kind of a nut—a Jesus freak.* Chances are they may not be overly enthusiastic about things of that nature.

I led weekly Bible clubs at several junior high schools when I was a Youth for Christ staff member in the mid-1960s. Most of these clubs met after school, usually at a church or home within walking distance of the school, and they were reasonably well attended. But there was one club that did not have a convenient meeting place near the school. I had to use a church bus to pick up the kids after school.

Each week when the school day was over, that old red and white bus (with "First Baptist Church" painted all over it) would be parked in front of the school, waiting for the kids. At the time, I had no idea why only two or three kids showed up. Dozens of kids at the school had said they wanted the club, but when it came time to get on that bus, they were nowhere to be found. In retrospect, I know that I was asking the impossible. To get on that funny-looking church bus in plain view of all their peers would have taken a lot more courage than most adults are able to muster.

It takes a great deal of boldness to be able to stand apart from the pressure of the crowd. And boldness takes time to acquire. Junior highers should not be made to feel they are less than fully Christian because they fear being different. They will have many opportunities during their lives to stand up for their faith and to move against the flow of group pressure, but these opportunities should come as a natural result of their growing Christian commitment. As junior high workers, we are better off helping kids to understand the meaning of their faith rather than forcing them to make impossible choices. When we know why we believe, we are able to make wise decisions.

On the other hand (there is always an "other hand"), junior highers can be encouraged to share Christ with their friends, invite these friends to church or to the youth group meeting, get involved in service projects, and make all kinds of public stands, so long as they feel reasonably secure doing so. It's not an all-or-nothing proposition. Every group and every individual is different, and you as the junior high worker must be sensitive to each person's needs and level of maturity. But generally it's best to avoid situations that might be excessively threatening to the early adolescent. There is no need to push them too hard.

Breaking Up Cliques: An Exercise in Futility

The clique is probably the most prevalent social structure of early adolescence. A clique is defined by Webster as "a narrow exclusive circle or group of persons." Eric Johnson defines it as "a small group of friends who stick together and shut others out."[5] While cliques are certainly not limited to junior highers, they do seem to take on great importance during the seventh, eighth, and ninth grades and cause a great deal of concern for junior high workers and teachers. Ideally, we want to foster a feeling of unity within the group, with each person expressing openness and friendliness toward everyone else, but that is very seldom attained in junior high groups. Even though most junior highers themselves regard cliques as unfair and wrong, they can't seem to avoid them. They are a major part of the social life of the early adolescent; they help in the transition from dependency on the family to the many upcoming associations outside the family. A junior higher would probably define the clique that he or she is a part of as "my best friends."

A common question asked by youth workers in the church is, "How can I break up the cliques in my junior high group?" The question arises naturally, since it is generally acknowledged that cliques are not desirable and are worth eliminating if possible. For a long time I had difficulty coming up with an answer that would satisfy me, let alone anyone else. I, like most junior high workers, have never had much success at breaking up cliques. I finally came to the conclusion that it was essentially useless and basically a mistake even to try. Good or bad, cliques are here to stay and are just a necessary part of growing up. They must be considered a given of early adolescence, and the junior high leader will have to work around them, rather than against them.

It is possible, however, to reduce the destructive or negative aspects of cliques in the junior high group. One way is to provide as many opportunities as possible for group interaction and participation. Anytime the group or class is doing something together—mixing, playing, talking to each other—relationships between cliques and individuals are more likely to improve. But when kids come into a meeting in their cliques, sit together in their cliques, listen to or participate in the program in their cliques, and then leave in their cliques, there is little chance that conditions will improve. Rather than lecture on the evils of cliques, it is best to involve the kids in a variety of activity-centered learning experiences that require communication and cooperation with each other, as well as in group games, and other chances to relate to those outside their little cliques. Plays, musical groups, parties and special events, camping trips, and so on are all useful as clique-reducing activities.

On the other side, small group projects or activities in which the group is allowed to choose its own members serve to encourage or strengthen cliques. Small groups are fine with junior highers, but it is usually best to use a random selection process to determine group members or to assign kids to groups not made up entirely of their close friends. Sensitivity is important here, of course. For example, usually it is not wise to separate a junior higher from all his friends. That approach is likely to backfire.

Watch for Those Who May Be Rejected

Within any junior high group there are usually a few kids who just don't seem to fit in. While this is not a problem for most junior highers, there are some who have real difficulty making friends and finding acceptance from others in the group. They may be rejected because of their appearance, personality, where they live, what school they go to, what their family is like, their abilities, interests, mannerisms, language, or perhaps just because they are new. The list of "reasons" a person might be excluded from the group can be endless, and they are undeniably unreasonable to the adult. Junior highers may seem cruel at this point, but, again, they are merely being typically junior high. Unfortunately, kids at this age discover that one way to satisfy their own need to feel accepted or superior is to find someone else whom they can look down on, ridicule, or simply ignore. It's a sad thing for a young person to be the object of this kind of discrimination.

Hopefully no junior high group in the church is so large that a situation like this is allowed to exist. You as a junior high worker should always be on the lookout for those in the group who appear to be rejected and try to help them fit into the total group if at all possible. While you can't force people into being well adjusted and having friends, to do nothing is usually not the best alternative. Kids should be made aware that one of the things that sets the Christian community apart from the non-Christian community is that no one is shut out. Everyone is accepted, regardless of how the world sees things. That has always been an identifying mark of the Christian.

Some junior highers who are rejected are quite capable of living with the situation without any sign of trauma or despair, and they may appear to accept their roles as loner with ease. We should, of course, be supportive and thankful for them. But this is not usually the case. Most young adolescents who have no real friends in the group and who are unhappy will, given the opportunity, simply leave and seek acceptance elsewhere. Those who, for whatever reason, must stick it out will more than likely have a very difficult time, and there may be damaging long-range results on their personality, faith, and ego-development. We should do whatever we can to find out why a person is being rejected and, whenever possible, provide help.

A few years ago in one of my junior high groups an eighth grade girl was being shunned by the other girls (and boys) in the group. It was having a negative effect on her, so we youth workers decided to see if we could help. We discovered that her parents had been divorced for quite some time and that she lived with her father, who had never remarried. One result of this was an apparent lack of guidance in personal hygiene and the social graces that are important for young ladies emerging into womanhood. One of our female counselors was able to spend quite a bit of time with this girl, helping her considerably. Of course, acceptance did not instantly occur just because she smelled or looked better, but gradually she did grow more comfortable as barriers between her and the others in the group were broken down. Her self-image began to improve as well.

There are no easy answers here, and the example above is not intended to be a model for similar situations. But the sensitive junior high worker will give special attention to kids who need it and will find creative ways to discourage the natural tendency for junior highers to discriminate against those who may be a little bit different. We can help by getting kids involved with each other more and by allowing needy kids to get more recognition by being allowed to do the things they do well. Sometimes it just means that we must be an especially good friend to every person in the group, thus becoming a common link between them all. In us perhaps they can see Christ, who is the One who is able to make us all one.

Notes

[1]Joan Lipsitz, *Growing Up Forgotten* (Lexington, Mass.: Lexington Books, 1977), p. 122.

[2]Alvin W. Howard and George C. Stoumbis, *The Junior High and Middle School: Issues and Practices* (Scranton, Pa.: Intext Educational Publishers, 1970), p. 34. Used by permission of Harper and Row.

[3]Jerome Kagan, "A Conception of Early Adolescence," in *Twelve to Sixteen, Early Adolescence*, ed. Robert Coles et al. (New York: W. W. Norton, 1972), p. 103.

[4]Eda J. Le Shan, *Sex and Your Teenager: A Guide for Parents* (New York: David McKay Co., 1969), p. 51. Used by permission.

[5]Eric W. Johnson, *How to Live Through Junior High School* (Philadelphia and New York: J. B. Lippincott Co., 1975), p. 199.

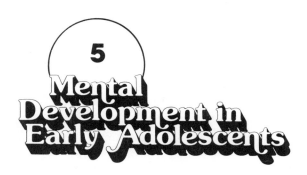

5
Mental Development in Early Adolescents

When I was a child, I used to speak as a child, think as a child, reason as a child; when I became a man, I did away with childish things. (1 Cor. 13:11 NASB)

—*Paul*

A real key to understanding junior highers is to take seriously the fact that early adolescence is a time of transition from childhood to adulthood—in more ways than one. Physically, the body changes so that it can function as an adult. Socially, we have seen how the junior higher's natural drive toward independence makes possible survival in the adult world. And while these definitive shifts are taking place in the physical and social areas, the young adolescent is in a period of equally exciting and disturbing intellectual change.

There are basic structural differences between the way a child thinks and the way an adult thinks, and, once again, we find that it is during the junior high years when most young people begin to develop adult understanding. The brain shifts gears, so to speak, and a whole new world emerges, much more complicated than before, yet wonderfully exciting. Prior to the age of eleven or twelve a child's understanding of reality is largely tied to what he or she can experience. But a qualitative change occurs coinciding with the onset of puberty, and this is more than just becoming more intelligent or learning more. The junior higher develops the ability to reason more logically, to conceptualize, to think abstractly, and to move from one abstraction to another. He can speculate on the many possible effects of something he wants to do. He can keep a lot of ifs in his head at one time and yet come up with an answer. These are all things he was unable to do when he "thought as a child."

Piaget's Theories of Cognitive Development

Most of the research in the field of cognitive development (how the mind develops) has been done by the highly respected Swiss psychologist, Jean Piaget. He has made brilliant observations of the thought processes of children, especially of their ability to think logically. He notes that intelligence, whatever that may be, does not increase at a steady rate but in spurts. Therefore, the conventional IQ score often is not an accurate measure of intelligence because people shift from one "stage" of thinking to a higher "stage" at different ages. What is especially significant for the junior high worker is that Piaget found that whereas the child reasons on the basis of objects (a stage he calls "concrete operations"), at some point during early adolescence the young person begins to reason on the basis of symbols and principles ("formal operations").

Piaget's stages of cognitive development are levels of thought, each one more sophisticated than the one before. People move from one stage to the next, never backward, as they mature. Piaget called the first stage the *Sensori-motor* period. It is best characterized by infants who do little or no organized thinking. They more or less only respond. Their perception of the world is obtained directly through their physical senses. By about age two, the child has learned that actions have physical consequences and that he and his environment are not the same.

The second stage is called the period of *Pre-logical* or *Pre-operational thought* and lasts typically from ages two to five. The thinking of children during this stage contains a magical element, in that children are not able to distinguish well between events or objects they experience and those they imagine. Although things are beginning to make sense, it is still their point of view that everything in the world revolves around them. Language and other symbols develop at this stage.

The third stage is called the period of *concrete operations.* (An "operation" is defined as a logical thought process.) Here people are not as ego-centered, but they still relate most things to themselves. Children between the ages of five and twelve are usually in this group. They learn to observe, count, organize, memorize, and reorganize concrete objects and information without losing the distinction between the real and the imaginary. They can figure things out for themselves and solve problems. The mind is much like a computer at this stage, processing information and making conclusions based on concrete data.

The fourth stage is called the period of *formal operations:* most people enter this stage between age eleven or twelve and age fourteen or fifteen if they are going to enter it at all. Some never do. But when a person does reach stage four, he or she is able for the first time to deal with abstractions, to reason about the future, to understand and construct complex systems of thought, to formulate philosophies, and to struggle with contradictions. Put another way, this stage gives one the ability to perform operations on operations—that is, to classify classifications, combine combinations, and relate relationships. One can "think about thought" and at the same time develop an awareness that knowledge itself is extremely limited.[1]

Graphically, Piaget's stages of mental development might look like this:

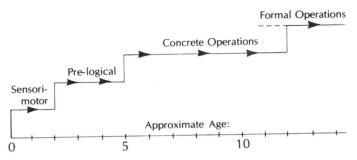

Recognizing the Differences

The differences between a stage three mentality and a stage four mentality are what is significant for the junior high worker in the church. These differences have a profound effect on education and ministry in the church in general as well. It is interesting that, according to studies, many Americans never reach adolescence in their capacity to think.[2] That is, they never learned to think abstractly. They never reach the stage where they reexamine their world, the people in it, what they believe, and themselves. It is important to know this, because to require a person who has not reached the period of formal operations to think in abstractions is to require the impossible.

Likewise, it is important to realize that a person who has reached the stage of formal operations can become extremely bored when forced to limit himself to a lower level of thought. No real intellectual challenge is offered in the church in which stage four people are asked to memorize religious facts or to accept everything that is taught without questioning. Much of our Sunday school curriculum is loaded with questions like "How long was Noah afloat in the ark?" rather than questions like "How could a God of love possibly justify the destruction of the earth's population at the time of Noah?" or "Could He do it again?" or "How could we learn from Noah's experience?" The latter questions would probably frustrate stage three thinkers but would be very stimulating for those in stage four. It is not sufficient merely to fill the heads of young adolescents with knowledge. They need to put it into practice and to "learn about their learning."

Many junior highers will know a great deal about the Bible, or about religion and the church in general, but will have a difficult time relating it to anything in a meaningful way. This period of transition from knowledge to living out their commitment will most likely be troublesome for them. This is probably one of the biggest problems with the traditional confirmation process in many churches. Junior highers attend confirmation classes and are asked merely to learn and then give back information. Once they have "learned it"—that is, the beliefs and dogmas of the church—and acknowledged an acceptance of it, then they are confirmed. Too often these are nothing more than rote memorization classes; they ignore the young person's need to question and to come up with a faith that is his or her own.

Joseph Adelson, a political scientist, made an observation concerning young adolescents that is pertinent to spiritual training:

> Just as the young child can count many numbers in series and yet not grasp the principle of ordination, so may the young adolescent have in his head many bits of political information without a secure understanding of those concepts which would give order and meaning to the information.[3]

Just as in political science, there are concepts essential to Christianity that must be understood in order to make it meaningful, for example, love (agape), ethics, morality, justice, reconciliation, trust, sacrifice, humility, the sovereignty of God, the struggle between good and evil, mystery, faith, hope, and the future. These are stage four concepts; they give order and meaning to the religious knowledge previously acquired. As a young person grows older, and the mind develops, these begin to come into focus. If they do not, or if they are withheld, there is no question that the young adolescent will lose interest altogether in religion and, more specifically, in Christianity.

The Questioning of the Early Adolescent

It is also at this age that kids begin to question much of what they have been taught. As young adolescents develop a new capacity for thinking things through and coming to their own conclusions, they find it necessary to reaffirm the learning they acquired from their parents, teachers, and peers. They want assurance that it is really true. They are quick to spot inconsistencies and contradictions that they were able to reconcile earlier without any problem.

Jerome Kagan cites an example:

> The fourteen year old broods about the inconsistency among the following three propositions:
> (1) God loves man.
> (2) The world contains many unhappy people.
> (3) If God loved man, He would not make so many people unhappy.
> The adolescent is troubled by the incompatibility that is immediately sensed when he examines these statements together. He notes the contradictions and has at least four choices. He can deny the second premise that man is ever unhappy; this is unlikely for the factual basis is too overwhelming. He can deny that God loves man; this is avoided for love of man is one of the definitional qualities of God. He can assume that the unhappiness serves an ulterior purpose God has for man; this possibility is sometimes chosen. Finally, he can deny the hypothesis of God.[4]

This kind of reasoning, regardless of its obvious oversimplification, is typical of how early adolescents privately work out their own set of values and beliefs. They have been told that sex (for them) is wrong, yet they find pleasure through sexual experiences. Is pleasure therefore wrong? They have been told that God answers prayer, yet they prayed and nothing happened. Why? Many junior highers are dismayed to find themselves facing an endless stream of problems like these that force them to make some adjustments regarding beliefs they hold at the moment. Left alone, the adolescent grows more and more skeptical, assuming that all religious truth is nothing more than wishful thinking. Sometimes this leaves the adolescent temporarily without a commitment to any belief.

These major conflicts pivot on the fact that old assumptions are challenged by new perceptions—perceptions created by the transition from concrete to formal operations. It is difficult to pinpoint when this shift occurs, but it is generally agreed that age has much to do with it. It has been said that the ideas of a twelve-year-old German, for example, are closer to those of a twelve-year-old American than to those of his fifteen-year-old brother.[5] But while this may be true, there are, of course, those slow developers, fast developers, or those who don't develop at all. This places an additional responsibility on the junior high worker, because the transition from stage three thinking to stage four thinking normally occurs during the early adolescent, or junior high, years. It is likely that there will be stage three people totally incapable of working at a stage four level and vice versa in the same junior high group.

The most obvious implication of this for the junior high worker is that junior high work is a very personal ministry. It only adds weight to the importance of building relationships with individual kids and getting to know them well. This doesn't mean that junior highers must be individually tutored, nor does it mean that they cannot be challenged with levels of thinking they are unaccustomed to. It does mean, however, that the junior high worker will be aware of kids who are having difficulty understanding certain concepts or who show an apparent lack of interest or seem bored. Likewise it is not necessary for one to become an "answer man," providing instant answers to every question. It is necessary, though, to be someone who is willing to listen and to encourage their questions. They need someone who will share their struggles.

Kohlberg's Stages of Moral Development

Another set of stages that we pass through on our journey from childhood to adulthood has been identified by Lawrence Kohlberg, a psychologist at Harvard University. He expands on Piaget's theories but with an added emphasis. His concern is with moral reasoning—how people think about right and wrong, truth and falsehood, good and bad. Kohlberg is interested in the "why" of moral reasoning, not just the content or the "what." People often arrive at similar conclusions or decisions but for completely different reasons. Kohlberg found that people go through fixed, predictable stages of moral reasoning, which explains how they arrive at moral decisions. This process is very similar to Piaget's stages of mental development. Kohlberg also found that we all go through these stages in a fixed sequence, and we never skip a stage. People, however, proceed at different speeds, and most people stop at a particular stage and proceed no further.

Kohlberg maintains that one's moral development can be seen (or measured) according to changes in (1) his concept of justice—right and wrong, (2) his ability to see things from another's point of view, and (3) the value he gives to human life. Each of these change as one progresses up the moral development ladder. Kohlberg identifies three "Levels" (major divisions) and six "Stages" (subdivisions).

Kohlberg's Stages of Moral Reasoning	Typical Age
Stage 0: Good is what I like	0 to 2
I. Preconventional Level Stage 1: Avoid Punishment Stage 2: You be nice; I'll be nice	 2 to 6 6 to 10
II. Conventional Level Stage 3: Good boy, Good girl Stage 4: Law and Order	 9 to 13 11 to 15 up
III. Postconventional Level Stage 5: Democracy, conscience, voluntary agreements Stage 6: Truth; Sacredness of life as a universal value	 adolescence (about 14) up rarely shown; fullest moral maturity

Kohlberg designates a "Stage 0," which is devoid of any moral reasoning. Practically, it applies only to infants, who simply know that "what I want and like is good." *Level one* (Pre-conventional) is entered by the young child at around age two. This level is typified by actions that occur without regard for others. All acts on this level are based on self. "Life" and "things" are not easily differentiated. At level one there are two stages: *Stage one* is based on avoiding punishment. Something is right or wrong based on whether or not it will hurt me. If I am frowned at, scolded, or hit, I don't do it. If I am rewarded, praised, or patted on the head, I do it. *Stage two* is the "What's in it for me?" stage. Good is whatever turns you on (the Playboy philosophy). People can be used for your own benefit. There is a sense of fairness and sharing, but it is based on how it will benefit me. This stage lasts usually up through age ten, however some people never go beyond this stage. Others regress to it at times, such as when undergoing stress.

Kohlberg's *second level* (Conventional) differs from the first in that here people submit completely to outside authorities, stereotypes, rules, and traditions. Again there are two stages included here: *Stage three* is the "way I'm supposed to be" stage. You do what the group considers right. Conformity to the wishes of the group (especially peers) is the norm. Good and bad is defined by the culture or by "society." Many junior highers are at this stage. *Stage four* is the "law and order" stage. What's right is what's legal. Law and morality are the same thing here. Obedience to rules or some outside authority is important here. This stage is usually entered at adolescence, but it includes the vast majority of adults in America as well. Many Christians (including pastors) are solid stage four people and probably will be for the rest of their lives.

The *third level* of moral reasoning (Post conventional) is based on what Kohlberg calls a "principled morality." Those who enter this level do so through a process of questioning the accepted rules and working out for themselves moral principles they hold to on the basis of their own convictions rather than because of some authority. According to Kohlberg, only about 20 percent of the population ever attain this level. Again, there are two stages: *Stage five* people would say that society is an instrument of man rather than the other way around. The majority rules. Law still fits in, but it can be changed if society considers it unjust. No one is better than anyone else, and each person has a responsibility to others. *Stage six* is Kohlberg's highest level of moral reasoning and stage six people are very rare. "Truth" is the determining factor in all decisions. Decisions are based on what is universally, logically, and ethically right. The interests of self and society don't matter. Justice is based on the interests of the least advantaged person in every situation. Human life and dignity is a sacred human value. Kohlberg identified Jesus Christ as definitely having been a stage six person.

So how does all this relate to junior high ministry? It is certainly not my intention in presenting Kohlberg's stages that you attempt to categorize people into this stage or that, or that you try to turn all your junior highers into full-fledged "stage sixers" by the end of next year. What is of relevance is that we need to be aware that the mind develops in an orderly fashion—not haphazardly, but according to a God-given pattern. One stage comes before the other and one leads to the next. The mind of the junior higher is not simply an empty jar waiting to be filled with knowledge, but it is itself growing in its capacity to assimilate information and to reason. We can be a vital part of the process by giving kids opportunities to nurture and to stimulate their growing minds. According to Kohlberg, it is only through struggle, through challenge, in which old beliefs are constantly tested and reevaluated, that people continue growing in their ability to think and to make morally responsible choices. There is no place to go but up.

Secondly, it is significant that Kohlberg's stages closely parallel Piaget's. It is impossible, for example, for people to pass beyond Kohlberg's stage four morality, that of law and order, until they have moved into Piaget's period of formal operations, when abstract thinking and a high level of questioning is possible. An understanding of this becomes very helpful when ministering to young people who are at different points of mental and moral development.

The Junior Higher and Adolescent Relapse

While both Kohlberg and Piaget have given us what appear to be smooth patterns for mental development, there are snags, especially when we are talking about junior highers. Some people have suggested that Kohlberg should have included in his system a "stage 4½" to accommodate what is often referred to as "adolescent relapse"—a giant step backward that occurs shortly after the onset of puberty.

It would seem logical that with newly acquired mental capabilities, junior highers would be anxious to excel academically and to put their improved brainpower to work, but the opposite is often true. It is a fact that for most young people the quality of schoolwork goes down drastically during the early adolescent years, and this is true in Christian education as well. Kids who may have excelled during the pre-junior high years often do quite poorly when they reach adolescence, much to the alarm of parents and teachers alike. This poses a frustrating problem for junior high workers, and this is another reason why so many people tend to avoid working with this age group.

The reason for this, of course, has to do with the emergence of the major distractions described earlier: the sudden physical growth, the rapid sexual development, the readjustment of relationships with adults and peers, and the surge toward independence. To expect a smooth academic performance when such turmoil is going on is to expect the impossible. It is not easy to make intellectual pursuits (Bible study, for example) fascinating enough to prevail over these urgencies. It is often not until the ninth, tenth, or even the eleventh grades that many young people develop a driving intellectual curiosity and a pleasure from dealing with ideas. This makes designing junior high curriculum a real challenge for everyone involved.

Motivation and the Junior Higher

Another question common among junior high workers is, "How can I motivate my junior highers to become more interested in spiritual things, or in the church, or in the youth group?" Obviously this is not an easy question to answer, since most junior highers are actually between motivations. That is, they no longer are motivated by a desire to please their parents or teachers, and they are not yet motivated by a desire to be better equipped for adulthood. Finding some way to motivate them in the interim can be difficult, to say the least. Some resort to force, not only in the physical sense but also emotionally. For example, kids are made to feel guilty for not performing up to prescribed standards. Bribery is also sometimes used: prizes, rewards, contests, gimmickery of all kinds serve as temporary motivation. More often than not the long-range effects of such approaches are disastrous.

It may be impossible to instill genuine motivation in kids, but perhaps I can offer a few ways to at least increase the chances that you will be able to maximize the interest level of the junior highers in your group. (1) If it is, in fact, other urgencies that distract junior highers from concentrating on academic, intellectual, or spiritual things, then make these things part of the curriculum. In other words, make it relevant. Kids will always be more interested in things that relate to where they are, what they are going through, and so on. If the subject matter has no practical application, it may be a complete waste of time. (2) Variety is important. Active, growing minds become bored easily. Use a variety of approaches and methods to cover a variety of topics. Don't get into a rut. (3) Involve kids in the learning process. Use as many activity-centered learning experiences as you can. Avoid lecturing when teaching can be done some other way. (4) Create a warm, friendly atmosphere in which learning can take place. If kids *feel* right away that they are accepted, that they are in a place that is fun, exciting, and happy, then motivation is not so great a problem. (5) Keep it personal. If each person knows that he or she is important, special, and cared for, they are motivated not to disappoint you. It is usually the kids who feel left out who are least motivated to participate and to learn.

Don't Hold Them to Their Decisions

As a final note, it would be wise to remember that junior highers are inclined to make a lot of mistakes while trying out their new reasoning and thinking capabilities. They realize that they possess the ability to make their own decisions, so they feel that it is necessary to make lots of them. Usually these decisions are made hastily, without being thought through, and they will more than likely wind up changing their minds a lot. They will sound very sure of themselves, certain that they know all there is to know about a particular thing. But they may be sure of something this week that they feel completely uncertain about next week. And they may volunteer for something today that they will "unvolunteer" for tomorrow. This kind of inconsistency is normal and is to be expected, for junior highers learn to make decisions through trial-and-error.

This can be another source of frustration for the junior high worker, of course, but it doesn't have to be. While it is important to help kids learn to be responsible for their decisions and to make wise choices, it is also important that they are not held to decisions they can no longer live with. They should not fear to make a decision because they are worrying that they may be stuck with it forever, good or bad. Instead they need an atmosphere that permits them to exercise their minds and to make the mistakes that lead to growth and maturity.

Notes

[1]Lawrence Kohlberg and Carol Gilligan, "The Adolescent as Philosopher," in *Twelve to Sixteen: Early Adolescence,* ed. Robert Coles et al. (New York: W. W. Norton, 1972), p. 154.

[2]Eric W. Johnson, *How to Live Through Junior High School* (Philadelphia and New York: J. B. Lippincott Co., 1975), p. 34.

[3]Quoted in Joan Lipsitz, *Growing Up Forgotten* (Lexington, Mass.: Lexington Books, 1977), p. 47.

[4]Jerome Kagan, "A Conception of Early Adolescence," in *Twelve to Sixteen: Early Adolescence*, ed. Robert Coles et al. (New York: W. W. Norton, 1972), pp. 93-94.

[5]Lipsitz, *Growing Up Forgotten*, p. 47.

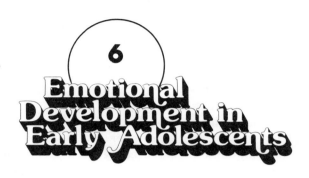

6
Emotional Development in Early Adolescents

By adult standards, junior highers are very emotional. Their emotions are completely unpredictable and extremely intense. Junior highers have been known to giggle uncontrollably during the first part of a youth meeting and then become despondent during the second half. And this occurs for no apparent reason. While this kind of behavior could be classified as typical, it is important to understand that there really is no such thing as a "typical junior higher" when it comes to emotions. It is possible to have within a group of fifteen to twenty junior highers those who are boisterous and loud and others who are quiet and shy. Still others in the group might be afraid, or self-critical, or confident, or angry; the list could go on and on. Emotionally, there are myriad peaks and valleys for the junior higher. They are on a kind of roller-coaster ride; they run the gamut of emotions and moods before they begin to settle down into a pattern, usually at around age fifteen or sixteen.

Unfortunately, the word *emotion* suggests agitation and excitement. There is often a tendency to think of emotions as strange forces mysteriously arising from the depths to seize the person and place him at their mercy. This extreme view exaggerates the dramatic and disturbing aspects of emotion and fails to acknowledge that much of the emotional life of junior highers is calm and constructive. A person can be quite emotional without flying into a rage, crying hysterically, or being silly. Emotions are always present, no matter what behavior we are displaying at the moment.

As we investigate the emotional side of junior highers in this chapter, keep in mind that emotional development is closely related to development in other areas of life. It is actually more of a secondary characteristic of junior highers rather than primary, even though there are some primary implications.

Emotional turmoil exists in early adolescents primarily because there is turmoil in the physical, social, mental, and spiritual areas of life also. Emotions are not foreign intrusions; they are more or less a reflection of what is going on in general in one's life, as well as a reflection of one's maturity. They hardly exist apart from these contexts. This is one of the reasons that it is practically impossible to make any predictions about how a person is going to integrate his emotions and his behavior, since each person responds to circumstances in his own way. One person may go through a great deal of stress in a given situation, while someone else may have no difficulty at all. Such is the case with junior highers. There are some early adolescents who seem to be sitting on an emotional powder keg, while others are able to take most everything in stride, and show an unusual amount of emotional stability.

Even though emotional development is a secondary characteristic of junior highers, their emotional inconsistency and unpredictability causes much distress and frustration for parents and teachers, simply because a junior higher's emotions are likely to be translated into some kind of action. In other words, they don't hide their emotions very well, even though they may try to. If a junior higher is feeling lousy, he will more than likely let you know about it in some "creative" way, and perhaps he will attempt to make everyone else around him feel lousy too. This tends to make life interesting (to say the least) for the junior high worker, and for this reason I will offer a few suggestions for dealing with the emotional development of junior highers.

Trial-and-Error Personality Development

At the outset of this chapter we noted that there are essentially two generalizations made about early adolescent emotional development. First the emotions of junior highers are characteristically unpredictable, fluctuating, and inconsistent. The second is that their emotions are very intense—what they feel at any given moment, they feel very deeply. We'll take Generalization Number One first.

Emotional unpredictability helps set junior highers apart from the rest of the human race. Adults and little children can normally be put into categories without too much difficulty. ("She's such a pleasant little girl." "Mr. Jones is a real happy-go-lucky sort of guy.") Junior highers, on the other hand, may be pleasant today and terrors tomorrow. I have had kids in my junior high groups who were unusually cooperative and enthusiastic one week and unexplainably belligerent and disruptive the next. I've also observed aggressive hostility and childlike submissiveness in the same meeting from the same junior higher. The junior higher who is talkative and open one moment could suddenly clam up altogether. Some people wonder if these kids might be victims of some form of schizophrenia.

These strange shifts in behavior are not limited to individuals, they are also found in groups. It is not uncommon for the dynamics in a group of junior highers to change from one week to the next. A particular lesson plan or program idea may be a smashing success on a given date with a given group of junior highers, but it could have been a complete flop if you had used it a week or a month earlier. It all depends on the mood of the group. With most junior high groups I have worked with, I have always had more concern (prior to a meeting, class, or social event) with how the kids were going to be (or respond) emotionally than with how many would show up or with how good the program or curriculum might be. There was always the fear that the group might be on a "downer"— uncooperative, on the defensive, or just plain nasty. As I said before, it makes life interesting for the junior high worker.

Adolescent psychology offers a reasonable explanation for this bizarre behavior, and this may be of some consolation. It certainly helps us understand what is going on, even if it doesn't alter the situation much. The explanation is this: In the process of adolescent development, junior highers are essentially "trying on" different personalities for size to see which one or ones suit them best. They will express a variety of emotions, feelings, attitudes, and temperaments to discover the range of reactions they get from others, especially their peers. If the reaction is favorable, the behavior may be repeated; if it is not, the behavior may be discontinued. This explanation may be an oversimplification, but it does help us to get a handle on what's happening. It is consistent with what we know about the primary tasks of early adolescence—these young people are making the transition from childhood to adulthood, and each one is trying to come up with an identity of his or her own. The personality, like the body and the mind, is being shaped during the junior high years, and it is probably in its most unstable period.

This is why it is not at all unusual for the early adolescent to be an extrovert one day and an introvert the next. He is only trying to see what he will be most comfortable with as an adult. A junior higher may try all sorts of personalities—the class clown, the tough guy, the brain, the teacher's pet, the quiet type, the spoiled brat, the flirt—before his or her own distinctive personality traits begin to emerge. He has not yet committed himself to a particular pattern, but he will be doing this only a few years later on in most cases. If a junior higher likes the feedback he receives from others by acting a certain way, this behavior will no doubt be continued. Conversely, negative feedback will usually act as a deterrent. Keep in mind, however, that negative feedback from an adult may very well be positive feedback to a junior higher: this tends to complicate things. The whole process is, in fact, a natural form of behavior modification.

By the way, the junior higher is never really aware of this subconscious trial-and-error personality-shaping process. He doesn't wake up in the morning and say to himself, *Yesterday I tried my warm and friendly personality; today I'll see how my mean and nasty one goes over.* It's not an overt kind of thing. It is all quite involuntary, normal, and necessary.

Have Patience, Don't Panic

As I mentioned earlier, this unpredictability in a junior higher's behavior pattern generates a good deal of anxiety for people who work with this age group. It is no easy task to adapt to the emotional ups and downs of junior highers week by week. It requires a considerable amount of patience, particularly when the behavior of the group is more negative than positive. The temptation in such situations is to punish them in some way, to give them a tongue-lashing, to call in their parents, or to threaten them with whatever might seem appropriate. In my experience as a junior high worker, I can recall times of panic, despair, or anger, and my impulsive actions at such times did more damage than good. If you lose your temper, or overreact in a negative way, it rarely accomplishes much. Usually it only gives the group some helpful feedback that they will undoubtedly file away for future reference; for example, now they know how to get to you. There is nothing wrong with being firm and strict and being honest about your feelings, but they do need to see maturity and consistency in their adult leaders as much as possible. Junior highers demand almost superhuman standards from the adults around them.

Rather than losing control, it is best to try to be as understanding as possible and relatively good-natured through it all, even when the kids are angry, belligerent, or uncooperative in return. The best advice is to have patience, make as few demands on them as possible, and just wait it out. There really is no better alternative. Sometimes it is a good idea to shift gears, to "go with the flow" or "punt." That is, it might be helpful in some situations to offer something that might be more compatible with the immediate mood of the group, rather than to force something on them they are not ready for.

Dr. William Sippel, a respected junior high school principal, gives some good advice on how to get along with this age group:

It takes a person with certain qualifications. He or she must have patience. It takes an understanding of these ‚youngsters. One must not overreact to their emotional manifestations, not get upset over them. . . . To deal with them, one should be emotionally tough, and yet have very humanistic qualities. If one of them tells you off, you have to be well-enough adjusted so that it doesn't make you feel insecure. They may accuse you of being funny-looking. If you have a long nose, they may yell that out. That could bother you.

We need people who are emotionally tough enough not to be bothered, yet human enough so that the next day you can give them the human help they need—as if nothing had happened. That takes a certain personality, almost the same kind the youngsters show, in a way— they have a lot of emotion, but are willing to make amends the next day.[1]

Discipline

The emotional ups and downs of junior highers will often create a real dilemma for the adult worker who is trying to be patient and understanding, yet at the same time remain firm and in control. How does a person maintain order and exercise discipline in a junior high group without being tyrannical or without alienating, humiliating, or hurting the kids? Obviously there is nothing to be gained by passively allowing complete chaos to exist in a youth group meeting. It is not usually in the best interest of the group to permit a few high-strung, disruptive kids to destroy a meeting or ruin a learning experience for others. A certain amount of discipline that is effective without being oppressive or stifling is necessary.

The question of discipline—how much, how often, and how to go about it—is usually a nagging problem for people who work with junior highers. Again, there are no easy answers here since every situation will require a little different approach. Also, each youth worker needs to have his own style, consistent with his personality and the personality of the group. When discipline is necessary, the important thing is to do it with consistency or with a predetermined standard that is fair, just, and understood by everyone from the very beginning. It should not seem arbitrary or impulsive. If kids have a good idea in advance that certain types of behavior will result in some corresponding consequence, they will not only try to avoid it, but also their dislike for the disciplinary action will be transferred to the "system" rather than to you personally.

This may mean that some basic rules should be established and everyone made aware of them in some way. For example, whenever I lead a discussion with a group of junior highers, I first lay down a few ground rules, like: (1) Only one person talks at a time. (2) Raise your hand if you want to speak. (3) If someone says something that you don't agree with or that you think is "dumb," don't yell, laugh, put them down, throw a tantrum, or pick a fight. Just raise your hand and you'll get your chance to speak.

It's not advisable to have too many rules, however. Rules tend to sound negative, and they put a damper on things. In addition, too many rules are difficult to enforce. One of the best ways to establish a few basic rules of behavior for a youth group is to create a "youth group contract" with the kids. At one of your meetings, announce or pass out a list of proposed rules that you have chosen in advance. (The more the better. It's good to include a few that border on the ridiculous.) Ask the kids for their suggestions as well. When the list is complete, divide the group into smaller units and have them decide which rules they want to keep and which they want to eliminate. They should keep those that they feel are fair, just, and necessary for the smooth running of the youth group.

Then have a discussion with the total group, with each smaller group sharing their conclusions along with their reasons. If you find that the kids have eliminated some useful rules or have kept some undesirable ones, you may express your feelings also. But the final decision should be left to a vote of the group. Usually they will do a very good job of selecting or modifying the rules they consider worthwhile and will be willing to honor. When all of this is completed, the rules can then be listed on a sheet of poster paper or parchment (like the Constitution) and then signed at the bottom by everyone in the group. It can be posted on the wall as a reminder that you now have a contract.

Of course, it may be necessary to add amendments as you go along, adding or dropping rules when the group agrees. Some rules may be more important than others. The idea is simply to predetermine standards for group behavior in advance so that you are never accused of being a dictator when you must administer some disciplinary action. Usually this procedure is more useful with large groups than smaller ones. Again, you should do what is best for your own group and what is consistent with your style of ministry.

Obviously the next problem is what to do when someone is guilty of disruptive conduct or of compromising the rules. Do you make them stand in the corner or make them do fifty push-ups? Do you report them to their parents or kick them out of the meeting? Do you embarrass them or put them down in front of the other kids? Do you hang them by their thumbs? Or worse?

As a rule, I have found it best to handle these problems individually with kids who consistently cause problems. This is where some personal counseling and honest sharing is extremely worthwhile. I have rarely had problems with kids whom I know well and have spent a lot of time with on a one-to-one basis. Because they value my friendship, they are less apt to disappoint me and put that friendship in jeopardy. One group has what they call "The Ugly Card System." It works this way: whenever someone breaks the rules or creates a problem, they are given one or more ugly cards, depending on the offense. These cards are much like traffic tickets, with predetermined penalties attached. One or two cards is usually a warning while a third, fourth, or fifth might result in some form of punishment. A person might have to stay and clean up after the meeting or be sent to the "ugly room" (use your imagination) while the youth meeting is going on. On the other hand, there may be ways for kids to get rid of their ugly cards by doing some positive things rather than being punished. Some junior high workers have found this approach to be effective, but it may not necessarily be the best way for you.

I'll toss out one more idea that we used occasionally when I ran junior high camps at Forest Home (southern California). It was called "The Mutt and Jeff System"—for reasons I'll never know. At the beginning of camp, the basic rules were usually announced (we only had two or three) and campers were informed that if anyone could not abide by these simple rules, we would arrange for them to be taken home. When we did have a problem camper, someone in authority (like the camp Dean) would sit down with the camper and his counselor and tell him there was no alternative but to send him home.

After the camper became thoroughly convinced he was in deep trouble, the counselor would then become the camper's advocate, and request a second chance, promising that he would change his ways. After some consideration the camper would be granted a reprieve. Usually this resulted in an immediately improved relationship between the camper and the counselor and almost always a positive change in the camper's behavior. I was involved in more than thirty camps with close to five thousand kids; to my knowledge, we never sent anyone home.

Remember that discipline depends a lot more on attitude than on a system. Junior high workers who worry about discipline problems will probably have more than their share. There is much more to be concerned about with your junior high group than enforcing rules and maintaining order. You can spend all of your time doing that. It is wise to know what you will do when a problem arises, but it is never helpful to dwell on the negative when working with kids. Keep it in the background. When a junior higher needs to be disciplined, try first to interpret the cause of his behavior and then decide how much you will interfere, if at all.

Behavior That Hides More Than It Reveals

People always wonder how an experienced junior high worker is able to function in what appears to be a state of total confusion. I can remember times when I would invite the pastor of our church in to speak briefly to the total junior high group, and invariably he would stand before the group and try to quiet the kids down and achieve total silence, but without much success. Frustrated, he would look in my direction, expecting me (nonverbally pleading with me) to *do* something, when really there was not much that I or anyone else could do. What he needed to do was to proceed and to ignore the ever-present stirring of the crowd. Despite all the noise, he would be heard, even though he might wonder how in the world that could be possible. Rarely can you tell how well you are communicating with a group of junior highers simply by noting the decibel level or by waiting to get positive feedback from the group.

Then there was the time I had spent several weeks with another group of junior highers studying and discussing the concept of *agape*—Christian love. We particularly concentrated on what it means to be the Body of Christ and how as Christians we should care for and love each other, striving for unity and harmony, and so forth. The kids were really into it, and I was confident that the way the group had responded to this material meant that our group was going to be the most loving, harmonious collection of junior highers in town. Unfortunately, it wasn't to be. Less than a week later, two of the dominant cliques in the group were at each others' throats (again), so one half wouldn't even speak to the other half. It was all I could do to prevent an all-out war. Apparently our study on love didn't make a very deep impression on them, I concluded.

Naturally, when things like this happen, you begin to wonder whether you are getting anywhere as a junior high worker or teacher. Normally you hope that you see results reflected in some kind of positive behavior, but with junior high kids, you just can't count on it. And it rarely has anything to do with how well or how poorly you are doing your job. Learning and growth in junior highers will be taking place even when their behavior seems to indicate otherwise. A junior higher's behavior will many times hide more than it reveals, so you can't really depend on positive behavior to measure your success, failure, or results. You will usually be disappointed if you do.

Every now and then at a conference or some other gathering a stranger will approach me with the statement, "You probably don't remember me, but. . . ." And they are usually right until they refresh my memory (and sometimes my memory is unwilling to be refreshed). It often turns out this person was in one of my junior high groups ten or twelve years ago, back when I was convinced beyond a shadow of a doubt that my efforts were a total loss. I am still humbled (and amazed) when one of these people expresses his or her gratitude for my ministry to them during their junior high years, and in some cases informs me that it was while in my group that he or she made a commitment to Christ that is still meaningful today.

It's highly improbable that junior highers will go out of their way to express that kind of appreciation until they have grown up and are able to reflect back on it. Of course, by then you may not be around; this makes junior high ministry a rather thankless job much of the time. Little children will come up and hug your leg. Adults will write thank-you notes, shake your hand,

and offer a word of encouragement or praise. But junior highers are a different story. You can knock yourself out for them and chances are they will leave—without a word. On the other hand, there will be times when they will shower you with praise and adoration, but it will likely vanish just as quickly and it appeared. The point is: don't depend on these kinds of results to keep you going. Hang in there anyway.

Intense Emotions

Let us now turn to Generalization Number Two. The emotions of early adolescents are very intense indeed. There really is no middle ground, no halfway mark. People, events, and things are either one extreme or the other—it is the best thing that ever happened or it is the worst. A thing is either superior beyond compare or so inferior as to be worthless. Many events and problems take on an importance out of all proportion to their actual significance. Broken romances, failure to make the team, or poor grades may result in depression so great as to lead to suicide. (Suicide, by the way, is currently the number two killer of youth today. Statistics show that in recent years, suicide has increased 20 percent; among adolescents, including junior highers, 200 percent).[2]

When a junior higher is happy, he is very often ecstatic. When in love, it is greater love than anyone could possibly understand. As an eighth grader in love, I remember plastering my bedroom walls from floor to ceiling with little cut-out letters that read "Marcia," and writing Marcia's name repeatedly over every square inch of my schoolbooks, homework papers, desk tops, tennis shoes, ball gloves, and anything else with space enough on it to write. Of course, when she gave me back my ring (covered with angora fur) I was heartbroken, but it didn't take long for someone else to take her place.

So it goes with the emotions of junior highers. Unlike older adolescents, they have little control over them. They fail to cope with their feelings realistically. They tend to surrender to them.

The junior higher's emotions can be explosive as well as deep. At times their discontent with themselves and others will express itself in anger, rebellion, or fear. And with junior highers, the anger and rebellion is likely to be physical rather than the verbal expression manifested by older adolescents. If something happens that the junior higher doesn't like—a person may bump into them or call them a derogatory name— they may lash out and throw a punch. Junior high and middle schools deal with considerable fighting between students, with the girls often being just as violent as the boys. Anger against adults often expresses itself in outbursts that end in tears. This anger is not focused as it is in high school students, who can express what they don't like in logical statements. The anger of the junior higher is highly emotional and usually short-lived. It is also quite difficult to deal with. You can't reason with an angry, tearful girl or boy. It's best just to wait it out.

Don't Play on Their Emotions

Early adolescents are highly susceptible to emotional appeals. They are fascinated by things that trigger a deep emotional response. Of course this makes them a prime audience for TV shows and films that play on emotions. They also like listening to music that is highly emotional, whether it be frenzied rock-and-roll or heart-rending love songs. Junior highers may also be lured into drugs and/or mysticism because of its emotional drawing power.

The temptation for the junior high worker is to take full advantage of this when attempting to produce desired results in the church. You can get junior highers to do almost anything if you get to their emotions. If you can make them feel guilty, afraid, excited, ecstatic, angry, or whatever, you can usually elicit the desired response. But like emotions themselves, these responses are usually very shallow and temporary. Emotions are not only intense at this age, but they are also transient, and anything based on them is also going to be fleeting. Of course, the classic example of this is the "mountain-top experience." The phrase was coined because camps and re-treats, often held in the mountains, have a way of becoming extremely emotional events (especially around the old campfire) with a lot of "decisions" being made. This is espe-cially true of junior high camps. But mountain-top experiences in general have a poor track record, unfortunately. Unless these experiences are based on more than just emotions, they aren't likely to survive when they are confronted with life on a more down-to-earth level.

This is not to say that emotions are wrong or that they should be discouraged or restrained in the church. Emotions will always enter into the picture whenever a young person re-sponds to the gospel, but it is not fair for us to play on those emotions. Be careful that invitations to accept Christ as Savior, to dedicate one's life to Christ, to volunteer for Christian service, and the like are presented without emotional pressure that may lead to only surface commitments.

Assure Them That Faith is Not Dependent on Feelings

One of the great mistakes of the Jesus Movement of the late '60s and early '70s was the use of phrases like "Get high on Jesus" and "Turn on to Jesus." These expressions came out of a youth culture heavily influenced by drugs and the need to "turn on" and to "get high." The young people who were coming to Christ no longer needed a drug-induced state of well-being; they found "a better high" (as they put it) in Jesus. I can appreciate that, but for many young people such a de-scription of the Christian life has been misleading and destruc-tive. The implication is that being high is a result or side effect of a commitment to Jesus Christ. If you are feeling high, Christ is there. If you aren't high, well . . . maybe you need to turn on a bit more.

Obviously, this kind of theology leads to problems. Our faith in Christ is never dependent on our emotional condition. For the Christian, we have the assurance that the Lord is with us always—even when we are in despair, feeling guilty, ashamed, angry, or afraid. We are just as much a Christian then as when we are feeling great. Of course, He is with us when we are "high," but not *because* we are high. God is constant. We change. We are the ones who are on the roller-coaster ride—sometimes up and sometimes down. Junior highers, especially, need to know that their faith is not dependent on how they feel. They are going to experience a variety of feelings, some good and some bad, and they need to know that Christ is always there and understands all of them.

Notes

[1]*Youth Report* (New York: Grafton Publications, January 1976), p. B1.

[2]James Reapsome, ed., *Youth Letter* (Philadelphia: Evangelical Ministries, Inc., March 1977).

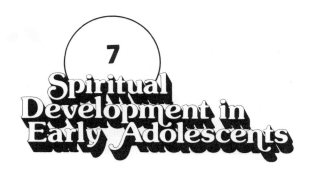

7
Spiritual Development in Early Adolescents

In this chapter we will look at a few key issues in the spiritual development of early adolescents. It is important to understand at the outset, however, the that spiritual dimension of life cannot be set apart from the rest of life as if it were an entity unto itself. It is not. One's faith touches every area of life—the physical, mental, social, and emotional. This is why we have devoted so much space to these areas thus far in this book. The "whole gospel" affects the whole person, not just the soul.

As a young person develops physically, socially, and mentally, these changes are going to have an effect on his or her spiritual life. Our purpose here will be to concentrate on a few selected problem areas for early adolescents and offer some guidelines that will help you maximize your ministry to them.

Doubting and Disbelief

A significant number of junior highers will reject or at least doubt their previously held religious beliefs. Many of the reasons for this have been discussed in detail earlier. Up to this age, most kids believe in God because their parents do. Their faith is somewhat of an inherited, hand-me-down variety that is no longer acceptable or adequate. Some young people find it necessary to discard this old faith altogether rather than to modify it or to try to live with it long enough to understand it more fully.

For others, faith in God is weakened by a growing mind and a newly acquired world view that discredits anything that cannot be empirically proven or does not make "good sense." They see their old view of religion as a world of make-believe and, like many once-cherished childhood myths, it is at least temporarily cast aside.

Still others will reject their faith because they are rejecting all authority in their lives and the baggage that goes with it. It is part of the process of breaking ties with the family and establishing an identity of one's own. It usually has very little to do with religion itself. The actual pros and cons of the gospel never enter into it at all. It is helpful to know this, because many times we attempt to "convince" nonbelievers that Christianity is true when that's not the issue at all. The problem frequently lies elsewhere. Christ may not be the one who is being rejected, it may be some authority figure instead.

Of course, there are always a certain number of junior highers who will have no doubts whatsoever (no serious ones anyway) and who will remain absolutely faithful throughout their early adolescent years, and for them we can be thankful. There will also be quite a few who have nagging doubts about their faith but are afraid to express them. This group is probably larger than the faithful.

It is advantageous to be aware of the doubts of your junior highers and to know why they may be experiencing pangs of disbelief or skepticism, but there is no need to attempt to eliminate their doubt. In fact, it really can't be done. Doubt is a necessary part of one's spiritual development, and the key is not to eliminate the doubt but to help the person to persevere. One must learn to doubt his doubts in much the same way he doubts his faith. It is also important to remember that God does not doubt you just because you doubt Him. John the Baptist expressed doubts about Christ even when he was imprisoned for his faith (Matt. 11:3). God understands our doubt and even our disbelief. These assurances can be most helpful to junior highers.

Early adolescents who may be in the process of rejecting their faith will still respond positively to someone who cares about them and who understands. The solution is not necessarily better curriculum, more weekend retreats, confirmation classes, or a special youth week commitment service. You can get a lot more mileage out of just being a friend.

The Problem of Faith in the Real World

A good many junior highers are far more threatened by their faith at this age than they are skeptical of it. Doubt and disbelief may not be a problem for them at all. Instead they discover that living the Christian life is just a lot more difficult than they had ever bargained for. They find that Christians who act like Christians are definitely in the minority among their peers and that to be overly religious is to risk one's acceptance and popularity. Some may feel that a choice has to be made between having many friends and being a good Christian, and the struggle over this dilemma is often quite painful. Some junior highers will in effect lead two completely different lives: the person who attends church, Sunday school, and youth meetings, and the person who is popular at school and at play. They find it almost impossible to allow these two lives to overlap. They consider them to be totally incompatible. This is why some junior highers would never even consider inviting one of their close friends to church.

Here we can see the importance of ministering the whole gospel to the whole person. Junior highers should not be taught that religious experience and religious truth are set apart from everyday experience and everyday truth. Many times kids are taught this in some very subtle, nonverbal ways.

When the church does not relate to the real world in practical ways, the church too develops a kind of split personality. We need to help early adolescents see that their faith is indeed compatible with their everyday lives and that being a Christian is not only something we *do* but something we *are.*

Programming and curriculum for junior highers should always have some practical applications and should relate to the present as much as possible. Early adolescents are not going to be helped a great deal by studying church history, eschatology (the doctrine of end times), or theological problems, all of which they have no interest in. The gospel must be seen as more than just religious propositions and other-worldly experiences.

Commitment and Failure

As a junior higher, my biggest problem was learning to cope with failure. To me, failure was a sure sign that my Christian commitment was going down the drain. In my early upbringing, failure to live according to the standards of the Scriptures, the church, and/or my parents was equated with sinfulness, and I was taught that good Christians do not sin. Or at least they don't sin very much. If they did sin, they were extremely minor sins more like little mistakes that were forgiven instantly or hardly worth forgiving at all.

This rather strange impression of the Christian life is often given to young people today, even in churches whose theology accepts and allows for the presence of sin or failure in the life of the believer. (Unfortunately, mine did not.) Commitment to Christ is so closely related to proper Christian behavior that the two are almost inseparable. A Christian is one who keeps the Ten Commandments, is obedient to parents, loves his neighbor, sits quietly in church, doesn't smoke, drink, cuss, and so on. The implication is that the successful Christian life is one that is free from sin and discouragement and doubt and all the rest.

As a young teen, I went to lots of camps and evangelistic-type services, and invariably I would make one more tearful commitment of my life to Christ, only to watch it disintegrate a few days later simply because I could not live like a "good Christian" should. When I would fail, and I failed a lot, I would just throw in the towel and give up on being a Christian altogether. (At least until the next evangelistic service.) Failure to me meant that I was not really committed, or at least not committed enough. It was an all-or-nothing proposition. *After all*, I thought, *even the Bible teaches that a person has to be either hot or cold. "If you are lukewarm, heaven forbid, it makes God vomit"* (Rev. 3:16, my paraphrase).

The problems inherent in this kind of thinking for junior highers should be obvious. A junior higher's life is going to be full of failure (see chapters three through six). Many times a young person at this age will almost be forced to reject his faith because he believes that there is too great a gap between what the Christian life demands of him and what he is able to give. Successful Christian living seems to be an impossibility. It is fitting and proper for the church to call Christians to the highest possible standards, of course, but this does not mean that we must sacrifice our junior high kids. Perhaps one of the most important messages that we can give junior highers is that commitment to Christ has nothing to do with secular notions of "success." Being a Christian does not require that we be successful. Commitment does, however, affect how we respond to failure. When we are committed to something, we hang in there and keep going even though we may fail miserably. Junior highers need to know this. They can and should be taught Christian principles for living according to the Scriptures, but they need to know that God does not expect perfection. Their perfection, after all, has been given to them through Jesus Christ.

A story is often told about the inventor Thomas Edison that may or may not be true. (I'll assume that it is.) Apparently it took more than nine hundred tries before he was able to make a light bulb that worked. In other words, he failed nine hundred times. Although he must have been discouraged through all of this, he stayed with it simply because he was committed to inventing a light bulb. He didn't give up.

The Christian life is certainly a lot like that. You don't get it right the first time or even the second. As the saying goes, Edison no doubt looked at each failure as just one more way not to make a light bulb. Maybe we should help our junior highers to see their failures as just one more way not to live the Christian life.

The Idealism of Early Adolescents

It is part of the early adolescent paradox that even in the midst of struggle, failure, and doubt, junior highers are extremely idealistic. They have a strong desire to be committed to something and to make their lives count. They are developing a keen sense of right and wrong and are quick to join in on projects that involve helping the less fortunate, even though they may lose interest just as quickly. It is not uncommon for junior highers to list as career choices occupations relating to service, such as doctor, nurse, misionary, social worker, and the like.

For this reason it is important they be given many opportunities to serve and to use the gifts God has given them. Their idealism, while it may be strong during the early adolescent years, will diminish over the years if not given expression, or it may be diverted into undesirable and destructive living. Junior high workers in the church should find as many ways as possible to channel the energies and enthusiasm of junior highers into service projects and other activities that allow them to give of themselves and to see the results of their efforts. They need to feel the significance and affirmation that such activities can give them.

Junior highers desperately need to know that they are important and that God can use them right now. They are not the church of tomorrow or next year's senior high group. This is an age when kids have deep feelings of uncertainty about who they are and what kind of person they are going to be. And it becomes even more difficult for them to find out what kind of person they will be when the church takes a baby-sitting approach toward junior high ministry and merely entertains them or shelters them during the early adolescent years. We should take every opportunity to nurture the idealism of early adolescents by helping them to recognize their value as a special person, created in the image of God, given many wonderful talents and abilities, and then treat them accordingly. This again requires a very personal style of ministry.

Some kids may feel that they were hopelessly short-changed when God was distributing the talents, gifts, and abilities necessary for becoming a "somebody" in God's scheme of things. A certain degree of discouragement might set in when they compare themselves to biblical or historical heroes of the faith, popular Christian celebrities of today, or adult Christians they know, like the pastor or youth director. Despite a genuine desire to accomplish much and to serve in some way, there is often the overriding fear that they are miserably unqualified and ill-equipped to do so.

Quite a few years ago, I heard a charming little parable that was a help to me when I was burdened with some of those same feelings of inadequacy. I have since passed it on to a good many junior highers, and for what it's worth, I'll pass it along to you.

There was once a little girl who wanted to become a great pianist, but unfortunately, all she could play was "Chopsticks." No matter how hard she tried, that was the best she could do. Her parents decided after some time to arrange for a great maestro to teach her to play properly. And of course the little girl was delighted.

When the little girl and her parents arrived at the maestro's mansion for the first lesson, she climbed onto the piano bench in front of the maestro's grand concert piano and immediately began playing "Chopsticks." Her embarrassed parents told her to stop (for no one ever played "Chopsticks" on a great maestro's grand concert piano), but the maestro encouraged her to continue. He then took a seat on the bench next to the little girl and with his right hand began adding some high harmony to what she was playing. He then added some notes with his left hand to round out the sound. The parents couldn't believe their ears. From this piano they were hearing a beautiful concerto, and the central theme was "Chopsticks."

Junior highers need to discover that little is much when God is in it, and that what they have to offer, even if it's only "Chopsticks" by comparison, is exactly what God wants to use.

The Importance of Models

Good models have always been important in the church. The apostle Paul often listed heroes of the faith he felt we should pattern our lives after, and he even went so far as to say "Brethren, join in following my example" (Phil. 3:17 NASB). Much of what a person learns about the gospel and about life in general is passed on not by words but by example.

This is an especially important truth for junior high ministry. Junior highers are dyed-in-the-wool hero worshippers and are easily led (or misled) by someone who captures their admiration and/or allegiance. In many cases this amounts to near worship of teen-age singers and actors, which in turn has given rise to the hundreds of teeny-bopper magazines and other products that take advantage of this situation. Almost every junior higher identifies strongly with someone he subconsciously (if not outwardly) patterns his life after. This ideal is often a public figure, but it could just as easily be someone closer. Howard and Stoumbis say this about models:

> This is the time for admiration and imitation of the hero figure, which makes it important that the proper figures for emulation are presented to the adolescent. While their parents and teachers are no longer likely to be the persons to be imitated and admired, partly because of their fallibility, familiarity and authority symbols, the early adolescent will still seek an older model to emulate—preferably one who is competent and successful by his adolescent standards.[1]

The extreme idealism of early adolescents causes them to hold most adults to almost superhuman standards. Because no one can fulfill their superhuman expectations, the successful person becomes the object of admiration, and unfortunately this is reinforced by our society, which rewards the competent and successful and rejects the failure. The result is a diversion of this healthy idealism and hero worship from the noble, authentic, and worthy to the undesirable, fake, and shoddy.

As junior high workers, we must do what we can to provide good models for early adolescents—not those who are superhuman and successful, but those who make good representatives of the gospel and of Christian values and who are able to inspire and challenge kids to high ideals.

Like it or not, we who work with junior highers are more often than not thrust into the position of model, simply because we are one of the few adults who have regular contact with the kids. They watch us, and we show them what adult Christians are like. The implications of this are certainly sobering. But it is also exciting when you think of the impact you can have on a young person at a critical stage in his or her life. It is a fact that much of the discipling we do with junior highers is not accomplished by simply teaching and programming, but by being the right kind of example and model for them. We must not contradict what we say with what we are.

Like the apostle Paul, we should always attempt to transfer the admiration and hero worship that comes our way to Christ (see 1 Cor. 11:1). Young adolescents should be shown that in the final analysis, only Christ is worthy of our admiration, trust, and esteem. Only He is truly superhuman, and only He will never disappoint us. And the best part of all is that not only do we know Him, but He knows us and is with us always.

Notes

[1]Alvin W. Howard and George C. Stoumbis, *The Junior High and Middle School: Issues and Practices* (Scranton, Pa.: Intext Educational Publishers, 1970), p. 34.

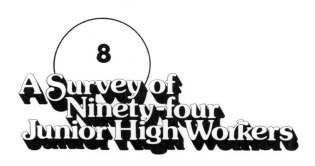

8
A Survey of Ninety-four Junior High Workers

I have always held that the best place for a youth worker to get good ideas on youth work is from another youth worker. With that in mind, I asked ninety-four junior high workers from twenty-four states to answer a few question about their particular junior high group and about junior high ministry in general. I received answers from a wide variety of people involved with junior highers, some professional, some lay people, some with big groups, some with small groups, from the city, the suburbs, the country, and from many denominations.

Despite the tremendous amount of diversity, there was a remarkable consistency in the responses that were given. It would appear from these surveys that most people, regardless of where they are from, share similar experiences and observations while working with junior highers. This chapter is a summary of these responses. In most cases, the most frequently mentioned answers appear first, with a few selected comments from the workers occasionally tossed in for good measure. The first few items in the survey give information on the kinds of people who were surveyed.

I should also add this disclaimer: The opinions expressed by these junior high workers do not necessarily express my views. Many of their comments are excellent and will stand on their own, but others are there for your amusement, or at least to show the range of responses that were given.

Number of Surveys:

Total	94
Males	53
Females	41

States Represented:

California (19)
Ohio (8)
Illinois (7)
Minnesota (7)
Pennsylvania (6)
Wisconsin (6)
Iowa (4)
Nebraska (4)
Indiana (3)
Oklahoma (3)
Texas (3)
Massachusetts (3)
North Carolina (3)
Arkansas (2)
Michigan (2)
Oregon (2)
Hawaii (2)
Washington (2)
New Jersey (2)
Florida (2)
Virginia (1)
Kansas (1)
Delaware (1)
Maryland (1)

Age:

Under 20	3
20-25	32
26-30	28
31-40	23
Over 40	8

Children:

No children of their own	56
Children under 10 only	20
At least one child in junior high	13
Children in high school, but none in junior high	4
Children college age or older	1

Education:

High school (5)
Some college or presently in college (20)
College graduates (36)
Graduate school (including seminary) (33)

Denominations Represented:

Presbyterian (21)
Baptist (16)
Methodist (10)
Catholic (5)
Episcopal (3)
Church of God (3)
Christian (3)

Denominations (cont'd)

Lutheran (3)
Assembly of God (2)
Congregational (2)
Wesleyan (2)
Nazarene (2)
Church of Christ (2)
Miscellaneous denominations or organizations (12)
Nondenominational (8)

Approximate Size of Churches Represented:

Membership between 0-200	15
Membership between 200-500	25
Membership between 500-1000	33
Membership over 1000	21

Location:

Rural	14
Urban	35
Suburban	43
Not stated	2

Income Level of Members:

Low	4
Mid-Low	2
Middle	68
Mid-High	8
High	12

Time in This Ministry:

Less than one year	16
One year	11
Two years	15
Three years	15
Four years	11
Five years	8
Six years	2
Seven years	3
Eight years	1
Nine years	2
Ten years	3
Ten - fifteen years	2
More than fifteen years	5

Paid?

Yes	42
No	52

Job Description:

Junior high sponsor (32)
Youth Pastor or Director
of Youth (21)
Junior High Director (14)
Sunday school/Church
school teacher (11)
Christian Education
Director (7)
Youth Group Assistant (5)
Pastor/Priest (2)
Camp Director (1)
Music Director (1)

Size of Groups (average attendance):

Less than 5	5
5- 10	15
11- 20	33

Size of Groups (cont'd)

21- 30	17
31- 40	6
41- 50	5
51- 60	5
61- 70	1
71-100	1
100-200	4
More than 200	2

Grades included:

Seventh, eighth, and ninth	40
Seventh and eighth	36
Sixth, seventh, and eighth	12
Seventh only	2
Eighth only	1
Ninth only	1
Fifth through eighth	1
Sixth through ninth	1

Boys?   Girls?

Total of all groups:
1541 girls
1357 boys
Groups consisting of

100% boys	0% girls	(2)
90% boys	10% girls	(0)
80% boys	20% girls	(2)
70% boys	30% girls	(1)
60% boys	40% girls	(7)
50% boys	50% girls	(38)
40% boys	60% girls	(19)
30% boys	70% girls	(16)
20% boys	80% girls	(2)
10% boys	90% girls	(1)
0% boys	100% girls	(6)

Question: *Why do you work with junior highers?*

I enjoy them. It's my favorite age group. I enjoy being around them. (21)

They are impressionable. A crucial time of life. I have a concern for this age group. (20)

I have the ability to identify with them. I possess an understanding of them. (18)

It's my job. (14)

Nobody else will. (9)

I was talked into it. (4)

I wanted the experience. (3)

It's challenging. (3)

God called me into it. (2)

• *Some selected comments:*

"Because I was once there myself and I can understand how important it is to know that someone cares for you and loves you, besides your parents."

"I like their enthusiasm and honesty . . . just the excitement of watching them grow."

"This is the age when kids form most of their decisions and attitudes."

"They challenge me to learn."

"At times I wonder about that myself."

Question: *Do you meet or work with the kids' parents at all?*

Yes (29)

No, or rarely (3)

Sometimes, occasionally, but nothing on a regular basis (35)

• *Some selected comments:*

"Mothers provide a weekly supper on a rotating basis . . ."

"We have a newsletter that is sent to the parents each quarter."

"They feel free to call us or talk to us about their kids . . ."

"We have a 'parents' potluck,' something on Mother's Day, and a 'fishing derby' for fathers and sons/daughters."

"They seem reluctant to participate."

"Yes, we visit in the homes regularly."

"We get input from parents when planning the year's program."

"We had a human sexuality program with the kids and their parents."

"About 85 percent of our kids are from broken homes. That makes it tough."

Question: *How many activities, classes, or meetings do you have per week with your junior highers?*

One per week (2)

Two per week (21)

Three per week (28)

Four per week (12)

Five per week (4)

Six per week (2)

One per week plus one special event per month (6)

One per week plus a biweekly one-on-one meeting (1)

Two per week plus one special event per month (2)

Three per week plus one special event per month (8)

Three per week plus biweekly mission trip/study project (2)

Two per month (4)

Two meetings and one special event per month (2)

Activities mentioned (in order of frequency):

Sunday school

Bible study

Fellowship nights

Youth meeting/Youth Club
Worship service
Confirmation/Communicants' class
Church basketball/volleyball teams
Parties, socials, special events
Sports Club, Game Days, recreation
Youth Council/Officers' meeting
Mission trips, service projects
"Koinonia"/Relational/Discipleship groups
Hand-Bell Choir
Dinner with choir rehearsal or fellowship afterward
Lunch Club during lunch hour at school
Crafts, drama, puppetry, music groups
"Boys Club"/"Pioneer Girls"

Author's Note:

Every junior high program I have ever seen has consisted of an assortment of big groups and small groups, with various quantities of each. The big groups tend to be designed to create that feeling of togetherness, excitement, fun, or bigness that is often needed with junior highers. They need to feel that they are a part of something reasonably big now and then. Small groups are usually best for maximum effectiveness in teaching/learning situations, Bible studies, discussion and sharing groups, and more personal encounter with kids. There is no set pattern, a right or wrong way to do it. Every junior high worker needs to custom-design his or her program to meet the needs of both the group and each member.

One idea that seems to work well is the "club" concept. Junior highers tend to like the idea of belonging to something, of being a member of a particular group. Many junior high groups have found it worthwhile to call themselves a club, complete with membership cards, T-shirts with an emblem or logo, dues, acceptance and/or initiation of new members, and the like. Of course, no one is refused membership, but still the feeling of joining something and being accepted by a group goes over well with the majority of junior highers.

One group in Los Angeles calls their weekly meeting simply "Thursday Night Club." A Denver group call theirs "CLICK Club" (Christ Living in Christian Kids). Quite a few groups use Greek letters—"Chi Rho," "Alpha Chi," "Alpha Teens"—or catchy names like "Sonseekers," "God Squad," "The Light and Power Company," and so on. Most groups are capable of coming up with an original name they like and feel comfortable with. Be creative.

Question: *Which activities do the kids seem to enjoy most?*

Social activities; recreation; anything active: bowling, skating, hayrides, picnics, parties (37)

Unstructured times of involvement: discussions, opportunities to present their own ideas, sensitivity and trust games, relational Bible studies, eating together, drama, crafts (23)

Youth fellowship; Youth Club meetings (18)

Educational times: Sunday school, Bible studies (5)

Music (concerts by Christian artists, etc.) (3)

Planning sessions (2)

Simulation games, educational games (2)

Camps and retreats (2)

Service projects (2)

• *Some selected comments:*

"Anything that gets away from the church building and super-structured classroom 'learning' experiences."

"If learning is made fun, with involvement, they enjoy it a lot and don't realize that they are really learning."

"They like anything that they plan themselves."
"Goof-off times."

Question: *What do you enjoy most?*

Small group sharing: support groups, discussions, rap times, informal sharing (18)

Social activities and active recreation (14)

Bible studies (14)

Youth Club/Youth Group meetings (9)

Unstructured fellowship times (6)

Service projects (4)

Retreats and camping (3)

Music (2)

Sunday school (2)

Liturgy (1)

• *Some selected comments:*

"Visiting them in their homes."
"Seeing decisions and results in their lives."
"The creative part—planning and preparation."
"Watching them grow, wrestling with who they are."
"I'm not enjoying any of it this year."
"I enjoy taking them on outings or having meetings at our house—they seem to feel less hostile, less on the defensive, more willing to tell how they really feel about issues that are important to them."
"Meetings when they are relaxed and behaved (which is very seldom)."

Question: *What is your greatest problem or frustration when working with junior highers?*

Discipline: noise, talking too much, etc. (17)

Parents: lack of interest, knowing how to deal with them,

their lack of concern, being poor examples, their non-involvement, their criticism (12)

Lack of support from church/senior pastor: financial, people to help, lack of space, general lack of concern (11)

My own commitment to junior high ministry; keeping my energy and enthusiasm (9)

Coping with the shifting moods and emotional instability of junior highs (8)

Negativism of kids: insulting each other, put-downs, not caring about each other, group injustices (8)

Lack of time (8)

Inconsistencies within the group: undependability of some, levels of maturity, etc. (6)

Passivity, lack of motivation (4)

Getting meaningful discussions going (3)

Getting the kids to plan the program and follow through (3)

Cliques and social pressure (3)

Lack of training and experience (3)

Finding good resources and curriculum materials (3)

Too many kids in the group (2)

Not enough kids, the group is too small, a low attendance (2)

Kids who use drugs (1)

Supersophisticated kids (1)

Encouraging loners to participate (1)

Finding men who will work with junior highers (1)

Kids lack confidence in themselves (1)

Lack of patience (1)

Co-workers who have opposite views on junior high ministry (1)

• *Some selected comments:*

   "It's frustrating to try to teach the kids and to help them when it seems as if they could care less. For example, we do things for them so they'll know right from wrong, and then they go ahead and do the things that are wrong anyway—smoking, drinking, foul language, sex, etc."

   "Developing an honest open relationship where there is mutual respect and the kid doesn't feel threatened. Controlling behavior while maintaining a positive attitude."

   "Never knowing whether you'll be talking to the 'sixth grader' or the 'high schooler' in that junior higher . . ."

Question: *What do you think is the greatest need of junior highers?*

The top ten:

1. Self-acceptance; self-confidence (43)
2. Relationship with God; a more meaningful, personal faith (25)
3. Peer-group approval and acceptance (13)
4. The need to belong; to know that they are not alone (12)
5. To learn to love, accept, and respect others (11)
6. Adult guidance; adequate role models (10)
7. To be independent, not dependent on peer approval or conformity (8)
8. To discover who they are; to use their gifts (7)
9. Honest communication; getting straight answers (3)
10. Fun and recreation (3)

• *Some selected comments:*

   "The need to cope with the many problems that arise from changing from a child to an adult; change in body, emotions, social awkwardness, freedom from parental ties and other . . ."

   "Challenge! They have to be motivated and challenged."

"Knowing how to deal with pressure from the 'world'—concerning drugs, dating, sex. . . ."

"Most of them have an identity problem. They don't know who they are or where they are going."

"To know they are loved when they feel so unloved and unlovable."

"To discover the shocking reality of Christianity in place of the do-it-right charade they know."

"To know they are OK just the way they are."

"Someone to confide in, answer questions, and love them."

"The self-confidence that comes from doing and creating successfully."

Question: *Any suggestions on how to meet those needs?*

On meeting the need of self acceptance:

"Involve them in planning and follow through of activities and programs."

"Listening to them and showing them that you love them by your actions."

"Tell them that they are important. Compliment them when they look nice or do something right. Use games and activities that help build self-confidence."

"Enjoy crazy times when we can all laugh and be free—not held back by inferiority or rejection."

"Provide settings where they can work out questions of self-identity and get positive reinforcement of their struggles and a healthy regard for differences in others."

On the need for a better relationship with God:

"Gear Sunday school lessons and programs toward the junior higher and his personal walk with the Lord; give practical instruction."

"Sharing your own personal struggles with them; being honest and letting them know it takes time to mature."

"Praying for them and watching out for them."

"More emphasis on the principles of God's Word to help them with decision making."

"Be a friend, not a preacher; help the kids discover their faith for themselves; let it be true for them."

On the need for peer-group approval and acceptance:

"Program situations that include everyone."

"Plan frequent outings to help them feel more like a 'family,' where everyone counts."

On the need to belong—to know they are not alone:

"Involve each person in the group activities; show love and concern for them individually."

"Learn their names; talk with them individually whenever possible; be interested in their non-church involvements as well as those at church."

"Create an atmosphere in which people are free to say what they think without being made fun of . . ."

"We've assigned adult couples a few teens as theirs to care for, to know, call on, spend time with."

On the need to learn how to love and accept others:

"Develop an awareness of each other; rap sessions, games that encourage working and cooperation with each other; helping them to see how they need each other."

"Develop a program of small groups—each with an adult advisor; these could be 'family' or 'care' groups, kids who keep in touch with each other."

"The only way to teach them love is to be an example and love them, which takes a lot of time and commitment."

"Retreats are good for this."

On the need for adult guidance:

"The junior high worker must be willing to give time, thought, and love to each person in the group."

"Put yourself in their shoes and share from your experience."

"Point them to other Christian adults who are good models."

"Involve parents; let kids see that their parents are human, too."

On the need to discover who they are:

"Value their presence by giving them opportunities to use their abilities."

"Make them do most of the work themselves; don't be critical when they fail."

"Don't pamper them. Challenge them with ways to use their energy and enthusiasm."

"Put youth members on church planning boards, committees, and such."

On the need for honest communication and straight answers:

"They should have mature leaders who prepare well and who have a knowledge of the kids' problems and also of the Bible."

"We should tell it the way it is and not the way we would like it to be. Be realistic with them."

On the need for fun and recreation:

"Program accordingly. In our group, we use a lot of skits and crazy things in most of our meetings. It puts the kids at ease. Also, we play 'capture the flag' every Saturday afternoon on the school playing field and the kids love it . . ."

Question: *How do you measure "results" in your ministry?* *

Feedback from kids themselves—conversations with them, surveys, their attendance and interest, planning sessions, etc. (23)

---

*Some responses contained more than one answer.

Watching kids grow as individuals—changes in their attitudes toward themselves (20)

Seeing improvement in their relationships to God—the way they verbalize it, questions, sharing their faith, putting it into practice (20)

How the kids relate to me as a friend—do they trust me and feel free to open up? (15)

Numerical growth or consistency in attendance (14)

A deepening involvement and interest on the part of the kids (14)

Watching how the kids relate to each other; improvement in group relationships (12)

Feedback from others—parents, staff, etc. (10)

Long-term results—high school or ten years down the road (9)

"Gut feelings" or self-reflection (9)

You don't (9)

• *Some selected comments:*

"I watch for small indications of change: in words spoken or questions asked."

"The enthusiasm of the kids; the reaction and feelings of their parents; the way they enter into community and school affairs."

"I watch them after they leave the group, and keep my fingers crossed . . ."

"By the smiles on their faces."

"When the group's dynamic changes from the small cliques and a few onlookers to one large caring community . . . then something's right."

"I don't. I measure my faithfulness to the job that God has called me to do. I see results through the kids' actions and relationships, but I don't place a great emphasis on them."

"I really don't know. Sometimes I get some good feedback from a kid whose life has been touched—that's super, but even no response doesn't mean we have failed."

"Results certainly include when a kid begins to think through his own faith for the first time. That's a lot of what it's all about."

"Very slowly."

Question: *What do you hope to accomplish as a junior high worker?*

This question produced ninety-four different responses, some of which were very similar, but the overall diversity was so great that it was not possible to do any grouping. Below is a representative selection:

"To help them develop into mature persons and Christians, and to help them cope with immediate problems they face."

"To help them practice and live out their faith at their level of ability . . ."

"To help this age group become comfortable in the church—that is, for each to recognize the church as a place that accepts them and cares for them."

"To help them through the problems that are unique to their own age group; to be an adult who cares; to show them that Christians can enjoy life as much as anyone; to love them even though they don't love themselves . . ."

"To help them make a personal commitment to Jesus Christ; to show them it is an adventure . . ."

"To help them become independent and be able to think for themselves."

"I want to become more vulnerable . . . less concerned about my programs and successes and more concerned about the kids themselves."

"To give them the best possible example in my own life; to let them know that I really care about them."

"I'd like to be able to see them still growing as Christians six or seven years from now . . ."

"Simply to be able to present the Word of God to them in a way they can understand."

"To help the kids grow up whole-ly alive and free to God and to the world."

"To let each junior higher find his own place in life."

"To help kids who are 'stuck in the middle' to understand that Jesus loves them in spite of their own searching and 'unacceptance' of self."

"To build a core group of kids who are in love with the Lord and with each other."

"To encourage participation in life. . . . To help the kids realize their potential as individuals. . . . To give them a solid moral base and to encourage them to make good decisions for themselves."

"Not much. If I've learned anything, it's that significant change occurs over a very long period of time. I just want my group to be one strong link in the chain . . ."

"I want to grow myself, through my own study and interaction with the kids. . . . Is that being selfish? . . ."

"To help youth to have a basis—experiential and content-wise—for making a decision for Christ; to communicate that the Christian faith has a lot to do with real life and real people, not pie-in-the-sky faith."

"I would like to think that my objectives have something to do with the well-being of the kids . . . but unfortunately, my main objective at this point is to keep my job."

"Primarily to help the kids to achieve a positive self-image through peer and home relationships; to give them an opportunity to explore life."

"To teach them care, responsibility, sensitivity, cooperation. . ."

Question: *List a few highlights of the past year in your junior high ministry.*

The responses to this question were generally lengthy and varied. There were many who listed specific activities that were successful, some of which were found on several surveys, like the "lock-in" (in which kids spend a weekend camping out inside a church building), camps and retreats of all kinds, creative things like banner-making, and dozens of other fun activities and service projects. Quite a few junior high workers, however, related incidents of a more personal nature, things not programmed but observed or experienced, like a noticeable change in a particular junior higher, specific acts of thoughtfulness by certain kids in the group, and so on. Listed below is a selected sampling of these interesting responses; they should give you an idea of the kinds of successes that some junior high workers experienced in the course of a year.

"There were two sessions where I knew I had the kids' complete attention—you could have heard a pin drop. I don't know what it was, but I felt that the kids were getting something out of my presentation. . . . Also, the conversations with the kids who show up early—one boy told me about buying a rug for his parents' anniversary from money he had saved. I was really impressed. Another highlight would be when some of the parents told me that their kids really like me."

"The concern some of the kids have shown for the older people in our congregation . . ."

"The kids put on an authentic family-style spaghetti dinner for the church and really came through, and when they prayed afterward there was such a spirit of unity and love . . ."

"A film we produced and taped about thanksgiving for our kindergarten classes."

"Watching them become more honest with themselves and about their relationship with Jesus Christ and God. . . . The look of surprise when they realize that God does work in their lives."

"A study class where we nailed sins (written on index cards) to a small cross and burned it in the fireplace. No one saw what the others wrote on his or her card. Only the junior higher and God knew; and burning it was to show Christ's forgiveness— He completely forgets them."

"When I see one of them in the hall or somewhere else and they seem happy to see me and say hello as a friend would."

"I find it most rewarding when a church youth council—officers of both junior and senior high youth groups plus two representatives from each grade (7 - 12)—meet with me once a month. We discuss problems, plan programs, and find ways for the youth to be more active in the church and the community. Young people on the council are very responsible and are very honest with me. Their comments are the best way I have of evaluating my youth ministry."

"When the most difficult kid in my group seems to really be learning something."

"Youth Sunday: The kids gave the service in church. I felt it to be the most meaningful church service of the year. It was great! They made up a skit about temptation and how to deal with it which was better than most sermons I've ever heard."

"Sue, who came to know Christ through a school friend. She stayed after class and bubbled with joy over her new discoveries. (She had been into drugs before her conversion.)"

"I just realized that they are capable of making their own decisions and planning much of their own programs and activities."

"A family activity—volleyball and slide show. The parents brought pictures of their kids when they were little for all to see. . . . A lot of fun!"

"Three junior high boys were committed to coming to 'Action Group' for nine weeks. During that time, they learned to open up with each other about subjects like divorce in their families, their sexuality, and general feelings about themselves. All conversations were confidential. Many deep-rooted feelings of anger, etc., surfaced, and I was able to deal with these in a safe and supportive environment."

"We had an all night 'lock-in' in the church in which each boy brought a friend. We had food, a radio, chess, Monopoly, even a poker game. . . . It was billed as strictly a fun event—very low key. We closed with a fifteen-minute service in the church sanctuary in which several boys willingly read from the Bible, lit candles, and so on. The boys seemed relaxed, and very much into the whole thing—confirmed as persons and open to the voice of God. I felt that the effort put forward was well worth it."

"An overnight canoe trip which gave us a sense of togetherness in adversity. . . . An Easter breakfast in which the kids served others."

"Watching kids who keep coming back even though they say they don't like church or religion or God."

"I gave instruction in the faith to junior high kids of a particular family, saw them through baptism and confirmation, and have begun to develop a great relationship (a lasting one) with the whole family. . . . I realized once again how marvelous it is for a person to hear his own name spoken. I made a special effort this year to get to know everyone's name and to use it."

"One that stands out: A girl in the eighth grade started coming to class but thought she was too good for everybody else. She was a typical 'teeny-bopper,' with her comb, etc. After about three weeks she brought a friend; this really surprised me since she seemed to have had such a negative attitude toward the group. Soon, they both were coming regularly and when one of them didn't, the other still showed up. It really made me feel good because apparently we had something to offer them both. And they are both eager to participate in class."

"A young man who had quit coming for six months has returned and is very involved and growing. . . . Also, a fishing trip with two of my boys."

"One of the fairly new kids, a girl, came up to me after our 'Sonseekers' meeting one night and asked my advice in solving a rumor problem at school. She keeps me up to date on how the problem is coming along, and told me that the advice I gave has helped her. It's a great feeling when kids will confide in you and actually trust you."

"The kids independently started making birthday cakes for each other this year."

"We have a ninth grade boy named Greg whom we nicknamed 'Jaws' because he would not stop yakking in Sunday school. He used to get my goat and both my wife and I thought he disliked us and wasn't learning a thing. Then last summer we went on a two-week mission trip to Mexico with thirty-five of the kids. We returned home on a Saturday and went to services on Sunday. On the following Tuesday, we received a note in the mail from Greg's mother which related that he saw us in church and told his mom, 'Hey, they are really all right!' She continued that we were the first adults to ever give Greg love and attention and that even though his behavior didn't show it, deep down he really loved us. That was a real highlight . . ."

"We organized a band and a singing group and now we play regularly at the senior citizens home."

"Just routine things that we do together—whether riding bikes, throwing a ball around, playing Monopoly, whatever, is neat because of the unity of this group. All of these combined, when one considers the 'typical' junior higher, have to be considered highlights."

"Cookouts, where the boys do the cooking! We have a 'best chef' contest. Also a pizza party in which they make the pizzas. They have to eat what they make."

"We had our first 'lock-in' and the kids were really surprised to find they could have lots of fun in the church!"

"The kids made a church banner for Epiphany and this was the first time they'd ever been made a part of anything . . . they were very proud and did very good work."

"A work project with an inner-city church caused quite a few to say, 'I'm really glad I went.'"

"A visit to a Greek Orthodox church; simulation games about food, famine, war, bargaining, and so on. The kids love them."

"As far as I'm concerned, the kids are the everlasting highlight. There are, of course, times when I'd like to shove them all down into the sewer, but then there are just as many or more times when they'd like to do the same with me! It is such a joy to watch them grapple with life and more often than not to come out on top. They grow so much, so rapidly, and in such varying patterns that becoming bored is hardly a problem."

9
Programming for Junior Highers: Activities and Games

Junior highers have a growing sense of humor and enjoy times when the group can just have a good time and laugh together. Of course, junior high humor is not generally of a supersophisticated nature; it can be better described as slapstick. In other words, they love the pie-in-the-face, practical-joke approach, and a junior high worker therefore has to be able to let his hair down and be a little crazy once in a while.

"Crowd breakers" of all kinds are especially good with junior highers for the purpose of providing a few laughs and for just having a good time. They are excellent to use during the first few minutes of any junior high gathering to get the attention of everyone and to start things off in a spirited, light-hearted way. The following crowd breakers are some of the best that I have used with junior highers, and they include group-participation activities, stunts, crazy games, and skits.

One word of caution: while junior highers enjoy stunts and slapstick humor, especially those with a "fall-guy"—in which a joke is played on someone—be careful to avoid situations in which someone is being made fun of or ridiculed for being clumsy, stupid, or whatever. Fall-guy stunts are OK and can be a lot of fun so long as the stunt is what is funny. The laughs should always be directed at the joke itself, not at the person involved. In that way, the fall-guy can laugh, too, and even feel somewhat heroic for being able to take it and be a good sport. In any event, use your best judgment and always be sensitive in these kinds of things. No one wants to be made a laughing stock, particularly if he or she is a junior higher.

The Banana Race

Ask for three volunteers who want to compete in a simple "eating contest." Blindfold them, and give each of them a banana. Explain that this is a contest to see who can peel and eat the most bananas in one minute. Before you say "go," secretly remove the blindfolds from two of them and ask them to go back to their seats. Then give the starting signal and the remaining person gobbles down the bananas, thinking he is competing against the other two people when actually he is just gobbling down a lot of bananas all by himself.

The Coordination Clap

This is a crowd breaker that you can use anytime, as many times as you want. It is always fun, gets good laughs, and involves everyone. The procedure is very simple. You move one hand up and one hand down (vertically), and the group must clap every time your hands cross in the middle. If your hands stop before crossing, then the audience must not clap. That is basically it. The fun is when you fake the group out by stopping just before your hands cross. Go fast, then slow, and point out people who goof it up. You may also stipulate that when anyone goofs, they are out of the game. Keep going until there is only one person left, and give him or her a prize.

The Cotton Ball Game

Have a person volunteer to see how fast he or she can pick up cotton balls with a spoon and place them in a bowl while blindfolded. Blindfold the volunteer, give him a spoon, and have him stand at a table with a bowl on it. Around the bowl, sprinkle a dozen or so cotton balls. (Let the volunteer see them.) After he is blindfolded, remove the cotton balls. Make sure he uses only one hand. The result is really funny to watch.

The Forty-inch Dash

This is a quick little game that is fun to play and to watch. Give three or more kids a forty-inch piece of string with a marshmallow tied to one end. On a signal, each person puts the loose end in his mouth and, without using his hands, eats his way to the marshmallow. The first person to reach the marshmallow is the winner.

The Hobby Game

Choose three boys in the room who have a hobby of some kind (any hobby). Explain to them that the group is going to ask them questions about their hobby and they are to answer without giving away their hobby, because later the audience is going to try to guess what these hobbies are. Then send them out of the room (supposedly so that the audience can think up some questions). While they are out, tell the audience that they are to assume that all three boys' hobby is *kissing*. (Regardless of what their hobbies actually are.) Call the boys back in, and ask them questions like the ones below. Their answers will be hilarious.

1. Who taught you your hobby?
2. How long does it take to do your hobby?
3. In which room do you perform your hobby or in what place?
4. What sound does your hobby make?
5. Is there any special training involved? If so, what?

6. How old were you when you first learned your hobby?
7. How do you get ready for your hobby?
8. What's the best time of the day to perform your hobby?
9. What do you wear when you are doing your hobby?
10. What sort of special equipment do you need?

The Hot Potato Game

The Ohio Art Toy Company manufactures a toy game called "Hot Potato" (also called "Spudsie") that is a great crowd breaker. You wind it up and pass it around the group, and after fifteen seconds or so, a bell rings inside the potato. Whoever is holding the potato at that time is the loser and receives a penalty of some kind, or is out of the game. When you pass it around, the following rules apply: (1) You cannot throw it, (2) You must take it if someone hands it to you, (3) If you drop it, it is still yours until you pick it up and get it going again, and (4) You may hand it back to the person who gives it to you.

Jawbreaker Crowdbreaker

Here's a crazy way to get kids divided up into groups for either a learning activity or game. Give each person a jawbreaker (candy) to suck on during the first few minutes of the meeting or event. Make sure that you distribute several different colors, with an equal number of each. After the kids have enjoyed the candy for a while, tell them to stick out their tongues and to find others who have the same color tongue as they do. The first group or team to locate all its members (with the same color tongues) is the winner.

Mad Libs

This game is a great crowd breaker for any age group and is available in book form from most book stores and stationery stores. It is a collection of stories, with certain key words left out, such as nouns, adjectives, and persons, and the audience supplies the words as they are asked for by the leader, without knowing anything about the story. The words the audience supplies should be as ridiculous as possible, and the leader writes them into the story as provided in *Mad Libs*. The results are always entertaining. The books are distributed by Pocket Books, Inc., 630 Fifth Ave., New York, and there are many editions of the game with titles such as *Mad Libs, Son of Mad Libs, Sooper Mad Libs,* etc.

The Midget Skit

This hilarious skit can be done by the junior high sponsors or by two of the kids who are reasonably creative. It works best when it is presented on a stage with a curtain and no lighting except for a spotlight on the midget. You will need the following props:

1. Table covered with a sheet or blanket
2. Man's long-sleeved shirt
3. Bermuda shorts
4. Shoes (large work shoes are best)
5. Paper bag containing one toothbrush, can of shaving cream, safety razor (no blade), banana, peanut butter and jam sandwich, cream pie
6. Towel lying on table

The lead person of this skit should be someone who can ad-lib reasonably well. He stands behind the table facing the audience and puts his hands in the shoes. He also wears the shirt but does not put his arms through the sleeves. Instead, his arms go straight down to the shoes. The shorts go around his arms just below the shirt and just above the shoes. The second person stands right behind the lead person and sticks his arms through the sleeves of the shirt. (You may have to cut the shirt to make this possible.) To the audience this looks like a very short person (a "midget") standing on the table.

During the course of the skit it will be necessary for the midget to shave, brush his teeth, eat, etc. The arms will be doing all the activity, and, of course, the arms can't see what they're doing. The movements should all be exaggerated by smearing toothpaste all over the lead man's nose, brushing his cheeks, sticking a banana in his eye, etc. The feet can also do some funny things by clicking heels together, running, etc.

The lead man's monologue can be hilarious. One good idea is to have the midget hitchhiking to some event (that you want to plug, perhaps). Explain to the audience that you are going to a certain place and need a ride. Several cars go by. Finally, one stops and the midget gets in (although he does not actually move anywhere). He talks to the driver of the car and explains where he is going and asks if he can shave before he gets there. He does and then asks if he can eat his lunch. After he eats his lunch he brushes his teeth, gets out of the car, and thanks the driver.

The midget can also be a girl. You can either change the costuming or use two girls and then supply beauty aids such as lipstick, mascara, etc. Then have a beauty class. The more creative and uninhibited the participants are, the more successful the skit will be.

Musical Hats

Pick six or more junior highers to stand in a circle, each facing the back of another person. In other words, they would all be looking clockwise, or all counter-clockwise. Five of the kids put on hats (or you can use paper paint buckets) and on a signal (or when the music starts) each person grabs the hat on the person's head in front of him and puts it on his own head. That way, the hats are moving around the circle from head to head until the next signal (or when the music stops). At that point, whoever is left without a hat is out of the game. Remove one hat and continue until there are only two kids left. They stand back to back, grabbing the hat off each other's head, and when the final signal is given, the one with the hat on is the winner.

Ping Pong Ball Blowing

Have two junior highers compete to see who can blow a ping pong ball out of a round bowl the fastest. Each person tries and is timed. Then, supposedly to make it even harder, they are to try it blindfolded. The first person does and is timed. Then the second person tries. But just before he blows, dump a cup of flour in the bowl. The results are really fun.

The W. C. Story

This is a crowd breaker that is simply read to the group. Give the following background information, then read the letter that follows:

An English lady visiting in Switzerland was looking for a room and she asked the schoolmaster if he could recommend one. He took her to see several rooms, and when everything was settled, the lady returned home to make final preparations to move. When she arrived home, the thought occurred to her that she had not seen a "W. C." in the place. (A "W. C." is a "water closet" or a bathroom.) So she immediately wrote a note to the schoolmaster asking if there was a W. C. in the place. The schoolmaster was very poor in English, so he asked the parish priest if he could help. Together they tried to find the meaning of the letters, W. C. The only solution they could find was "Wayside Chapel." The schoolmaster then wrote the following letter:

My Dear Madam:

I take great pleasure in informing you that the W. C. is situated nine miles from the house in the center of a beautiful grove of pine trees surrounded by lovely grounds.

It is capable of holding 229 people, and it is open on Sundays and Thursdays only. As there are a great number of people expected during the summer months, I suggest that you come early, although usually there is plenty of standing room. This is an unfortunate situation, especially if you are in the habit of going regularly. It may be of some interest to know that my daughter was married in the W. C., and it was there that she met her husband. I can remember the rush for seats. There were ten people to every seat usually occupied by one. It was wonderful to see the expressions on their faces.

You will be glad to hear that a good number of people bring their lunch and make a day of it, while those who can afford to go by car arrive just on time. I would especially recommend your ladyship to go on Thursdays when there is organ accompaniment. The acoustics are excellent, and even the most delicate sounds can be heard everywhere.

The newest addition is a bell donated by a wealthy resident of the district. It rings every time a person enters. A bazaar is to be held to provide for plush seats for all, since the people feel it is long needed. My wife is rather delicate so she cannot attend regularly. It is almost a year since she went last, and naturally it pains her very much not to be able to go more often.

I shall be delighted to reserve the best seat for you, where you shall be seen by all. For the children, there is a special day and time so that they do not disturb the elders. Hoping to be of some service to you.

                                              The Schoolmaster

Games and Recreation That Include Everyone

It really goes without saying that junior highers have lots of energy and enjoy playing games—the more active, the better. Good games are not only fun, they are also healthy and give kids a chance to use their physical and mental skills and to relate to others in a community-building atmosphere. It is always good to include a regular time for recreation in the junior high program of the church whenever possible. A Saturday or Sunday afternoon of games in the park or a Friday evening "fun and games night" in a gym or in the church fellowship hall will nearly always be one of the most popular activities with the kids.

The most important thing, of course, is to choose the right

games. While there will always be a few favorites that the kids enjoy more than others, it is best to provide a variety of games—different games that offer new challenges and new ways to have fun. Games should be playable by anyone, regardless of ability, and the competition involved should make games exciting, without becoming an end in itself. Winning should be almost irrelevant or anticlimactic to a good game. The important thing is that everyone has a good time playing the game.

I highly recommend to you another book which I have coauthored with Mike Yaconelli and Denny Rydberg called *Fun-N-Games* (also published by Zondervan, 1977). It is an up-to-date encyclopedia of games and contains over four hundred games of all kinds, most of which can be used successfully with junior highers. It also includes an extensive Christian philosophy of recreation that expands and details some of the ideas I've presented in this book. Most of the game suggestions below also appear in that book and are especially good with junior high groups.

American Eagle

This is not a co-ed game. Guys and gals should play separately. All players form a line. They choose one who stands thirty feet or so away (in the middle of a field). When the whistle is blown, players start running toward the one in the middle of the field. That person tackles one (or more if he can) and has to hold him down and say "American Eagle" three times. The rest of the players on the other side of the field must now run through two guys to get back to the original side. This keeps up until everyone has been tackled and all are in the middle of the field. There are no more guys to run across. Give a prize to whomever lasts the longest.

Amoeba

Divide into teams and tie a rope around the team at their waists. To do this, have the team bunch up together as closely as they can and hold their hands up in the air while you tie the rope around them. After they are tied, they can race to a goal and back. Unless they work together and cooperate as a team, they will go nowhere. This is a fun game for camps and outdoor activities.

Balloon Basketball

There should be an equal number of people on the two teams. There can be any number of players on a team, so long as the teams are equal. Arrange your chairs in rows in the following manner. One team faces in one direction, the second team faces the other direction. The two single rows of chairs on each end should face inward.

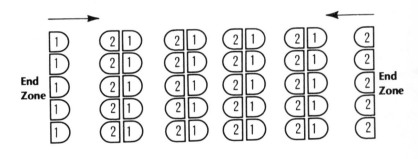

After all the players are seated, toss a balloon into the center. They cannot stand, but they must try to bat the balloon to the end zone they are facing, using only their hands. As soon as the balloon drops into the end zone over the heads of the last row of people, the team facing in that direction wins two points. If the balloon goes out of bounds, just throw it back into the center. The game can be to twenty points, or it may end after fifteen minutes of play.

Balloon Stomp

Everyone receives a balloon and a piece of string. Each person blows up the balloon and ties it to his or her ankle with the string. When the game begins, kids try to stomp and pop everyone else's balloon while keeping their own intact.

Barnyard

Give each person a folded piece of paper with the name of an animal written on it. The person is not to say a word or look at the paper. He is to sit down and await further instructions. (To ensure equal teams assign the same animal to every sixth person.) After everyone is seated, the group is told to look at their paper and when the lights are turned out they are to immediately stand up and make the sound of their animal:

1.	Pig	4.	Chicken
2.	Horse	5.	Duck
3.	Cow	6.	Dog

As soon as they find someone else who is making the same noise, they lock arms and try to find more of their teammates. When the lights come back on, everyone sits down. The team most "together" wins. For added fun, give one guy in the crowd the word *donkey* on his paper.

Bedlam

This game requires four teams of equal size. Each team takes one corner of the room or playing field. The play area can be either square or rectangular. On a signal (whistle, etc.), each team attempts to move as quickly as possible to the corner directly across from their corner (diagonally) performing an announced activity as they go. The first team to get all its members into its new corner wins that particular round. The first round can be simply running to the opposite corner, but after that you can use any number of possibilities: walking backward, wheelbarrow racing (one person is the wheelbarrow), piggyback, rolling somersaults, hopping on one foot, skipping, crab walking, etc. There will be mass bedlam in the center as all four teams crisscross.

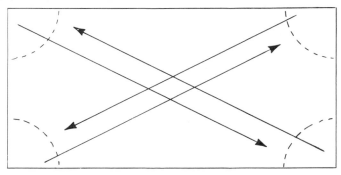

Birdie on the Perch

Have players pair off and get into two concentric circles. The boys should be in the outside circle and the girls should be in the inside circle.

When the whistle blows, the boys' circle begins moving clockwise and the girls' circle moves counter-clockwise. When the leader yells "Birdie on the perch!", the boys stop where they are and get down on one knee. Each girl must quickly locate her partner and sit on his knee and put her arms around his neck. The last couple to get into this position is eliminated. The game continues until only one couple remains.

Broom Hockey

This game may be played with as many as thirty or as few as five per team, but only five or six are actually on the field at one time from each team. Two teams compete by running out onto the field at a whistle, grabbing their brooms, and swatting a volleyball placed in the center through the opposite goal. Each team has a goalie, as in ice hockey or soccer, who can grab the ball with his hands and throw it back onto the playing field. If the ball goes out of bounds, the referee throws it back in. The ball may not be touched with hands, or kicked; it may only be hit with the broom. Score one point for each time the ball passes between goal markers.

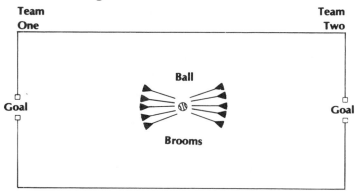

For a team with thirty members, for example, have them number off by sixes, which would give you six teams of five members each. Let all the "ones" play a three-minute period, then the "twos," etc.

Broom Twist Relay

Teams line up in normal relay race fashion. At a point some twenty or thirty feet away, a team captain or leader stands and holds a broom. Then the game begins, one player from each team runs to his team leader, takes the broom, holds it against his or her chest with the bristles up in the air over his head. Then, looking up at the broom, the player must turn around as fast as possible ten times, while the leader counts the number of turns. Then the player hands the broom back to the leader, runs back to the team, and tags the next player, who does the same. Players become very dizzy, and the results are hilarious.

Bucket Brigade

Each team lines up single file with a bucket of water on one end and an empty bucket on the other. Each team member has a paper cup. The object of the game is to transfer the water from one bucket to the other by pouring the water from cup to cup down the line. First team to get all the water to the empty bucket wins.

Domino

This is a great game for larger groups that is not only fun to play, but fun to watch as well. It's also easy to play and requires no props. Teams line up in single file lines with teams parallel to each other. There should be the same number of people (exactly) in each line, and everyone should face the same direction, toward the front of the line. On a signal (whistle, etc.), the first person in each line squats, then the next person (behind him) also squats, then the next person and so on all the way down to the end of the team's line. (You cannot squat down until the person immediately in front of you squats first.) The last person in line squats and then quickly stands back up again, and the whole process repeats itself, only in reverse, with each person standing up in succession instead of squatting. (Again, you cannot stand up until the person behind you first stands up.) The team that completes this first, with the person at the front of the line standing, is the winner.

The effect of this visually is much like standing dominoes up side by side and pushing over the one on the end. Each domino falls in succession. This game is much like that, only the dominoes first go down, then back up again. It works best with at least twenty-five or so in each line (the more the better). Have the group try it several times for speed.

Ha Ha Ha

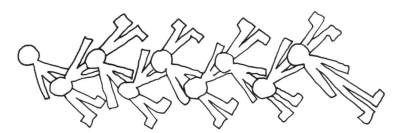

This is a crazy game that is good for a lot of laughs (literally). One person lies down on the floor (on his back), and the next person lies down with his head on the first person's stomach, and the next person lies down with his head on the second person's stomach, and so on.

After everyone is down on the floor, the first person says "Ha," the second says "Ha Ha," the third says "Ha Ha Ha," and so on. It is to be done "seriously," and if anyone goofs it, the group must start over. It's hilarious.

Hustle

For this game, everyone has to really *hustle*. You need something that everyone can scramble through or under; like under a bench, through a drain pipe or large cardboard box or old car, under a table, etc. The team lines up single file on one side of the bench (as an example) and on "Go!", each person hustles under the bench and gets back in line as quickly as possible. Each team has an impartial counter who counts the kids as they pass under the bench. The object is to see how many kids can hustle under the bench in one minute (or some other time limit). Each team gets a try and goes one at a time.

Inner Tube Relay

Each team divides into couples. The couples should be of the same sex, rather than boy-girl couples. Each team then lines up in different corners of the room, if possible. Inner tubes (one for each team) are placed in the center of the room. Each couple must run to the inner tube, and squeeze through the tube together, starting with the tube over their heads and working it down. The first team to have their couples complete the stunt are the winners.

Super Sack Relay

Divide into teams with ten people on each team. Have a brown paper bag for each team with the following items in each:

Jar of baby food
Green onion
Can of cola (warm)
Raw carrot
Piece of cream cheese (wrapped in wax paper)
Box of Cracker Jacks
Peanut butter sandwich
An orange
An apple
A banana

On signal, the first member of each team runs to his bag and must eat the first item he pulls out. Sponsors should make sure items are satisfactorily finished before the person goes back and tags the next member of the team. First team to finish its sack wins.

Tetherball Jump

Here's an old game that groups really enjoy. Have ten to twenty players form a circle. You get in the center of the circle with a tetherball (a ball attached to a rope about eight feet long). Take the rope in your hand and begin making circles with the ball, about six inches off the ground. The circle of players then moves in closer and each person must jump over the ball as it passes by. You keep going around and around, getting faster and faster until someone goofs. That person is then out, and the game continues. The last person to remain in the circle is the winner. As the game progresses, you may make the ball go faster and/or higher off the ground. Two leaders (ball twirlers) are recommended to take shifts in the center if you get dizzy easily.

Socials and Special Events

Junior highers have a lot more free time on their hands than most older teens, so it's not a bad idea to program accordingly. Unlike high schoolers, they don't drive, have weekend jobs, date, or have school football and basketball games to go to.

They stay home a lot and just complain about not having anything to do.

Taking advantage of this, many junior high groups plan at least one special event each weekend—on a Friday or Saturday night, during the day on a Saturday, or maybe on a Sunday afternoon. Other groups limit their social activities to only one per month or maybe twice monthly. Regardless of their frequency, junior highers really enjoy getting together with their friends just for fun and they love to get away from home whenever they can. Socials and special events can and should be an integral part of any well-planned junior high program.

There are many possibilities for a special event: a party at someone's home, a trip to an amusement park or to the beach, going bowling, skating, or miniature golfing, or taking in a good movie or concert. In addition to these ideas, there are dozens of unusual and creative fun activities you can create yourself like the ones suggested below. There is an infinite number of possibilities, most of which are effective ways to provide quick relief from the usual routine of youth group programming, and also to provide good opportunities for both outreach and evangelism.

Outreach is many times a primary goal of the activity-centered junior high group. Sometimes it is almost impossible to get new kids to come to worship services or youth group meetings, but in most cases they will come out to a social or special event. It is there that these kids can be introduced to the group for the first time in a much less threatening, more casual atmosphere where everyone is relaxed and is just having a good time. This does not mean, on the other hand, that you should turn every social into an evangelistic meeting. Never lock the doors and pass out the Bibles. There is nothing wrong with just having fun together and going home without the traditional devotional, speaker, or other attempt to spiritualize the event. Many times this is neither necessary nor appropriate.

The other obvious benefit of the special event is fellowship.

Group social activities are excellent for encouraging youth group unity, establishing new friendships, and for just keeping enthusiasm high.

But regardless of their purposes, the important thing is to use variety and creativity when planning socials and special events. Never be content with doing the same things over and over again. There will be certain activities the kids enjoy and are worth repeating, but it is best to give them new experiences and to avoid letting yourself get into a rut as much as possible. With that in mind, here are some special event suggestions that are truly out of the ordinary and that have been used successfully by a number of other junior high groups.

Action Scavenger Hunt

This is a creative variation of a scavenger hunt. Each person (or team) receives a list similar to the one below and goes door to door as in a normal scavenger hunt. At each house the person at the door is asked to perform one of the actions on the list. If they comply, that item can be crossed off. The team with the most crossed off at the end of the time limit, or the first team to complete the entire list, is the winner. Only one item may be done at each house.

1. Sing two verses of "Old MacDonald."
2. Do ten jumping jacks.
3. Recite John 3:16.
4. Name five movies currently playing at local theatres.
5. Yodel something.
6. Run around your house.
7. Start your car's engine and honk the horn.
8. Take our picture.
9. Whistle "Yankee Doodle" all the way through.
10. Say the Pledge of Allegiance.
11. Give us a guided tour of your backyard.
12. Autograph the bottom of our feet.

13. Say "bad blood" ten times very fast.
14. Burp.
15. Do a somersault.

Banana Night

This is a special event that will really make your group go bananas. The theme is bananas and everyone is encouraged to wear yellow, or brown (slightly overripe), or green (not so ripe). After everyone arrives, you stick "Chiquita banana" stickers on them and divide into teams (which you can call "bunches" instead of teams) and play all kinds of games that involve bananas, like:

1. *The Banana Relay:* Four teams of equal size form a square, with each team lined up as one side of the square.

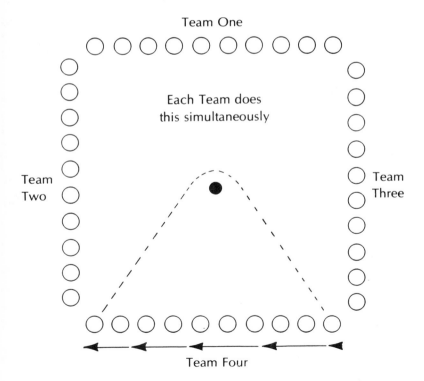

Everyone sits on the floor or on chairs. At the center of the square is a chair or some other object, but no one sits there. The first player at the left end of his team line is given a banana. At the signal, that player runs around the center chair without touching it and back to the right end of his team line. In the meantime, all of his team members have moved up one seat, leaving a vacant chair at the right end. After taking that vacant chair, the first player passes the banana up the line. When the end player receives it, he then runs around the center chair, sits in the new vacant chair, passes the banana down the line, and so on. Each team repeats this process until all the players are back in their original positions and the first player once again has the banana. He then eats the banana, regardless of the condition it is in, and the first to do so is the winner.

2. *Un-Banana Race:* Individual competition in which players get a bottle of Seven-Up and a banana. The object is to see who can first eat the banana and then drink the Seven-Up in the shortest time. The results are hilarious.

3. *Great Banana Race:* Each team gets a bunch of bananas placed a certain distance away from the team. One at a time, the players run to the bananas, eat one, and return to the team, tagging the next person in line. The first team to eat all the bananas wins.

4. *Pass the Banana:* Each team sits in a circle with their feet toward the center. At the signal, a banana is passed from person to person by cradling the banana with the feet. If the banana is dropped, the person who dropped it becomes the beginning of a new circle so the banana must be passed completely around again. Each team is timed (starting over, of course, if the banana is dropped), and the team with the shortest time wins.

5. *Doctor the Banana:* Each team is given a banana, a knife, and several toothpicks. Within an agreed time limit, each team performs "open banana" surgery. This is done by

carefully peeling the banana and slicing it into four equal pieces. These pieces are shown to the judge to verify the cut. Then the patients are "cured." This is done by putting the banana back together again, peel and all, using toothpicks where necessary. The winning team is the one with the most cured banana.

6. *Couples Banana Eat:* Each team selects a couple to represent them. Place a peeled banana with one end in the boy's mouth and the other in the girl's. The first couple to eat the banana without using their hands, wins.

7. *Bobbing For Bananas:* Bananas float, so throw a bunch of bananas in a tub of water and bob for bananas.

For prizes give away those ball-point pens known as "Bic Bananas" and for refreshments, serve—what else?—banana splits!

The Bike Blast

This is a fun special event that can involve the entire junior high group in an exciting day of bike activities. Everyone meets at a place large enough (paved) to handle all the bike games below, and of course, everyone should bring a bike. (Furnish bikes to kids who are unable to bring their own.)

1. *100-Yard Dash:* Race by categories—size of bikes, age, etc.

2. *Backward Race:* This should be an optional event, for those who can ride their bikes backward.

3. *Figure Eight Race:* Set up a figure eight track and contestants ride through it one at a time for the best time.

4. *Obstacle Race:* You could call this a "bike slalom." Set up a track with obstacles—mud, trees, cars, or anything to make the riding difficult. Again, the race is for the best time.

5. *Bike Jousting:* Bike riders ride toward each other in parallel lanes. Each rider gets a water balloon. The object is to ride by your opponent and hit him or her with your water balloon without getting hit yourself. Winners advance.

6. *The 100-Yard Crawl:* Bikes must travel in a straight line to a finish line one hundred yards away. The idea is to go as slow as possible. If a rider touches a foot or any part of his body to the ground (trying to maintain his balance) or goes off course, he is disqualified. The last person to finish wins.

7. *Bean Bag Toss:* Bike riders ride past a garbage can placed twenty feet or so away from the bicycle lane, and try to toss a bean bag (or a water balloon) into the garbage can without losing their balance or stopping. This can also be done with a baseball tossed at bowling pins or standing wooden blocks; or it could be done with basketballs on a regular outdoor basketball court. You simply try to shoot a basket while riding your bike.

This event can be wrapped up with a bike hike to a local park or to someone's home for refreshments and some group singing. The kids will love it.

Frisbee Festival

This is a good special event for the beach or for an open field where you have plenty of room. All you need is a supply of Frisbees (available everywhere). Divide the groups into teams and then play the following crazy Frisbee games:

1. *Frisbee Relay:* Team members line up with about twenty feet or so between them. The person on one end of the line gets the Frisbee and on a signal tosses it to the teammate closest to him, who then tosses it to the next person, and so on to the end of the line, and then back again. The first team to complete this wins.

2. *Frisbee Distance Relay:* For this one, you need lots of room. The first person on the team throws the Frisbee as far as he can. The next person picks it up where it lands and throws it again from that point even farther. The next person throws it again and so on. The team that gets the Frisbee the farthest away is the winner.

3. *Frisbee Toss:* Teams of two stand about ten feet away from

each other. (There should be two lines of players who stand this distance apart.) On a signal, a Frisbee is tossed from one to the other. Then both partners take one step backward, and the Frisbee is tossed again. Another step backward, the Frisbee is again tossed, and so on. If the Frisbee is dropped, that pair is out of the game. You must stand in one spot when throwing and catching. Whoever lasts the longest wins.

4. *Team Toss Frisbee:* Two teams line up parallel to each other and about twenty feet apart. The teams face each other and the first person on one team tosses the Frisbee to the first person on the other team, who then tosses it to the second person on the other team, and so on down the line. The thrower's team gets a point if the catcher drops the Frisbee, and the catcher's team scores a point if the thrower tosses the Frisbee beyond the reach of the catcher, who must keep his feet planted. There should be a neutral judge for this game.

5. *Singles' Competition:* There are many games designed for individual competition that you can play with Frisbees. Players may throw for distance, throw left-handed (or opposite-handed), throw for accuracy (through a tire or at a target), throw the "boomerang" shot for accuracy on the return (the Frisbee is thrown up and at an angle so that it will return), the "hot dogger" shot (any spectacular shot—sort of a "Frisbee Freestyle," which is judged for originality), and so on.

6. *Other team games:* You can play football, soccer, baseball, and even golf with Frisbees by just making up your own rules and by being a little creative. Have fun!

Late Great Skate

Here's a special event designed to put new life into the old roller skating party. First of all, rent a roller rink for your own private use. Usually you can get one for a flat rate plus skate rentals. Also, make sure you have the freedom to plan your own skating program, rather than being confined to the normal "All Skate," "Couples Only," "Grand March" kind of thing. You might want to consider an all night skate that starts around midnight and goes until dawn. Roller rinks are easier to get at such a ridiculous hour.

The basic idea is to play all sorts of games on skates. Many of your favorite games can be played on skates, giving them an added dimension of fun. Races, relays, ball games, all can be done on skates. Just be sure that the games are not too rough, to avoid possible injuries.

Some sample roller skating games:

1. *Rag Tag:* Everyone gets a rag that hangs out of their back pocket or out of their pants. On a signal, everyone starts skating in the same direction. The object is to grab someone else's rag without having yours taken by another skater. Once your rag is gone, you are out of the race. Awards are given for most rags grabbed by one person and for whoever stayed in the longest.

2. *Obstacle Course Relay:* Set up an obstacle course for the skaters. The first team to have each of its members skate through it (one at a time) is the winner.

3. *Triple Skate:* Have everyone skate around the rink in threes. No passing is allowed. On a signal, the skater in the middle, or on the right or left, moves up to the next threesome. This is good as a mixer.

4. *Scooter Race:* Have one kid down on his haunches who is pushed by another skater. Set a number of laps for the race.

5. *Tumbleweed:* Have all the skaters squat when the music stops or when the whistle blows. This will tire them quickly.

6. *One-legged Race:* Skaters race with only one skate. The other foot is used to push.

7. *Run the Gauntlet:* Girls line up in two parallel lines and the boys skate between them with balloons tied to their seats. The girls try to pop the balloons with rolled-up

newspapers. Another way to do this would be to have clothespins (3) fastened to each boy's back, and the girls try to grab the clothespins as the boys skate by. Awards are given to the girl who grabs the most clothespins and to the boy who lasted the longest.

8. *London Bridge:* Two skaters stand opposite each other, grab hands, and form a bridge for other skaters to skate under. Each team then lines up and, on a signal, begins skating under the bridge. Once under the bridge, each skater circles around and goes through again, as many times as possible before the time is up. There should be a counter standing by the bridge.

There are many other possibilities, of course. For breathers, you might want to show some films or serve sandwiches and refreshments.

Superstar Special

Here is an activity that is fun to do anytime and that can involve all of the kids in some really crazy competition. It is patterned after the "Superstar" events held on television, featuring famous athletes competing in a variety of events to determine who is the best all-around athlete. Normally, there are ten events (you may have any number you want).

Each participant selects seven events to compete in. If you prefer, you can make everyone compete in all of them, but by giving kids their choice of seven, it helps to equalize things a little bit. In TV's version, only the top three contestants in each event score points, but you may want to allow the top ten in each event to receive points. For example, first place would receive ten points, second place would get nine points, and so on. If someone were to take first place in all seven of his events (very unlikely), he would score seventy points total.

It is best to choose events that do not give a huge advantage to kids who are athletically inclined, older, smarter, or whatever. This way everyone has a chance, and the competition is more fun for everyone involved. Some sample events:

1. Water balloon shot put (for distance)
2. Shoe kick (hang shoe loosely on foot and kick it for distance)
3. Baseball hitting (use volleyball or have kids hit wrong-handed)
4. Sack race (in gunny sacks)
5. Paper airplane throwing (for distance in the air; everyone makes their own airplane)
6. Dart throwing (at dartboard or at balloons)
7. Stilt race (for best time)
8. Joke telling contest or dramatic reading contest (judged)
9. Taco eating (who can eat the most in a given time limit)
10. Frisbee throwing (for distance or accuracy)

Of course, you can create your own events to fit your situation. The kids move from event to event and record their scores. At the end, whoever has the highest score (total points) is declared the superstar and is awarded an appropriate trophy or prize (the crazier the better).

10
Programming for Junior Highers: Creative Learning Strategies

It is no secret that one of the worst ways to teach is to depend solely on the lecture method. The best way for a learner to learn is not by merely sitting and listening, but by also actively participating in the learning process. Today there is a growing interest in the church in what is commonly termed "experiential education," and this gradual shift in educational methodology has been a healthy one. Traditionally the emphasis has been on teaching: training teachers to teach. Today there is more concern for learning itself: finding better ways to encourage the learner to learn. Teaching is something that teachers do; learning is something that learners do. Findley Edge wrote:

> The responsibility for learning rests with the learner. If the learner doesn't want to learn, if he is unwilling to expend some effort in order to learn, then nothing the teacher does will make much difference. . . . By our emphasis on teaching (which is important), we have given the wrong impression to the learners. We now need to place the emphasis, and the responsibility for learning where it belongs—on the learner. . . .[1]

Experiential education takes the old "learn and do" principle (you learn something and then do it) and reverses it to "do and learn." That is, you do something and learn by doing it. It is based on the presupposition that the only learning that lasts and significantly affects behavior is that which is self-discovered. Of course, this approach does not rule out the lecture method altogether. It is useful for conveying from one person to another a large quantity of information in a relatively short amount of time. What experiential education forces us to do is to think creatively and to consider alternative methods that involve the learner more directly and hopefully produce better learning.

One of the primary strategies of experiential education is the simulation game. A simulation is essentially defined as a simplified model of some real-world system. A game, on the other hand, is any contest (play) among adversaries (players) operating under constraints (rules) for an objective (winning, victory). A famous example of a simulation game is the popular Parker Brothers game, "Monopoly." While the game is played primarily for fun, it is also a replica of a miniature society with its own economy and laws, very similar to a real world society. Valuable learning (about buying and selling, the rich versus the poor, cooperation and risk, etc.) can take place while the game is in progress. Learning is a by-product of the game and happens almost without the players realizing it.

There are many group games usable with junior highers in the church that operate in much the same way. Kids engage in play or in some kind of structured activity that produces learning about a particular topic. Learning, then, is almost totally self-discovered, wherein lies the value of this kind of activity. There are numerous suppliers of prepackaged simulation games, as well as a variety of books and periodicals offering extensive simulation gaming theory plus ideas. The following ideas were created mostly by youth workers and are excellent for use with junior highers.

The Awareness Game

Begin your session on awareness as follows. Have one person in the group go out of the room for a short time (pick someone who isn't easily embarrassed). Then ask the rest of the group to describe what the person was wearing. Be as specific as possible. Then bring the person back in and let everyone see what he or she was wearing.

Most groups will remember very few specifics about the clothing worn by the chosen person. From this you can talk about the shallowness of our everyday contacts with people. This can lead into a discussion of our ability as Christians to perceive others' needs and can also show that perception is the first step in ministering to a need. This also points out that noticing things about others is something that must be worked at. This discussion could also lead into Christ's perception of needs, how He relied on God the Father for help in this area, and what this means for our ability of perception.

The Body Life Game

This game is a good way to demonstrate the need for the New Testament concept of cooperation and unity within the body of Christ. To set up the game, divide the entire group into five smaller groups, which will symbolize various members or parts of the body. Each group should be named accordingly, i.e., Eyes, Hands, Ears, Feet, and Mouth.

The object of the game is fairly simple. The five groups, all members of the same body, must work together to perform various tasks before life dies. To symbolize Life, someone can be locked in a trunk or box and a road flare can be lit nearby. When the flare goes out, Life will be considered dead. The only way that Life can be saved is to complete the tasks that lead to the trunk key. (Flares are usually good for about thirty minutes.)

Each of the five groups should be equal in size and labeled in some way (different color armbands or signs hanging around their necks, etc.). In order to complete the tasks, each group may function in only the way that it functions in a normal body. In other words, and Eye will not be able to hear and an Ear won't be able to see. Eyes can only see and Ears can only hear. Therefore, everyone except the Eyes must be blindfolded.

When the game begins, the blindfolds go on, the flare is lit and the group gets its first task. The instruction for that task is written and presented to the Eyes, who whisper it to the Ears, who likewise whisper it to the Mouths, who then verbalize it to the rest of the body. Whenever the group must go anywhere, the Feet carry the Eyes (the only ones who can see) and the remaining members of the body must follow behind in single file, holding on to each other's waists. The Eyes in this case are allowed to speak, giving directions to the rest of the body.

The tasks may be relatively simple. Three or four good ones are enough. A few examples:

1. Crackers and juice should be fed to the Mouths by the Hands while being guided by the Eyes. The Feet will then carry the Ears to (place) followed by the rest of the body in single file.

2. The Ears will be given a number (by the leader) between one and ten. The Ears must then hold up that many fingers for the Eyes to see, who then tells the Mouths, who shout it to the Hands and Feet. Everyone must then get in smaller groups of that number of people. The Eyes may help everyone get together. (This can be repeated.)

3. Splints and bandages can be provided that the Hands should use to splint one arm and one leg of each of the Feet, guided by the Eyes.

The above tasks are only samples. It is best to work out a few things that your group can do to fit your situation. The last task should lead to the envelope containing the key to the trunk. The Hands must use the key to open the trunk, again guided by the Eyes and carried there by the Feet.

The discussion that follows could include the following questions:
1. Talk about the game and how each part of the body did or did not function.
2. Did everyone do their part?
3. Why didn't some people get involved?
4. Relate this to Paul's description of the "body" (1 Cor. 12).

The Day Church Was Blown Up

The following game (or fantasy experience) is an exercise in establishing priorities in the church and in helping young people to determine their own goals and attitudes toward the church. This works best at a camp or retreat when the kids are away from the church. The procedure is as follows:
1. Print up the following letter and place copies in envelopes, with each kid's name on an envelope:

Dear_____,

As an authorized agent of the Gibralter Insurance Company, it is my duty to inform you that at approximately 11:00 p.m., Friday evening, your pastor called together all of the adult members of your church for a special prayer meeting. It is my unhappy duty also to inform you that at 11:10 the Air Force accidentally dropped a bomb on the church and completely destroyed it. You and the members of your small group will now have to make some important decisions.

You are now the only surviving members of your church, and this makes you legally responsible. There is an insurance reimbursement of approximately one million dollars to cover the building and grounds. However, in order to qualify for this money you must show to us how you plan to reorganize your church. I for one, will be interested to see if you organize in a traditional manner or in a unique way. I have been told that there are no ministers available from the church body, so you will have to provide your own.

I wonder whether you will want to hire other people to do the work in the church or whether you will do it yourself. I wonder whether you will pay salaries to yourselves. I expect you to build a new building. Will you? What will it look like?

These are all questions that must be answered in the near future, but for now we would ask you to complete these forms so that we can settle your insurance claim as quickly and easily as possible. Thank you, good luck!

1. What will be the name of your church? (Will you keep the name as it is, or will you change it?)
2. Who will be the members of your church and what are their roles and salaries, if any?
3. On the other side of this sheet, make an organizational chart of your church.
4. Describe briefly the type of building you plan to construct or your reasons for not having a building. (You don't need a building to receive the insurance reimbursement.)
5. Describe your new church's ministry. What will be your basic purpose?

2. Have a surprise mail call and distribute the letters.
3. Break into small groups and begin planning your new church.
4. Regroup at a specified time for sharing or organizational charts and discussion. Ask if the suggestions would really work and whether or not they could be incorporated into the present church structure.

Dear Abby

This is a simple yet effective way to give kids the opportunity to really minister to each other and also to provide you with insight into the concerns and problems of individuals in your junior high group.

Each person is given a piece of paper and pencil. The kids are then instructed to write a "Dear Abby" letter. They should think of an unresolved problem that they have and explain it in letter form to a newspaper columnist like Abby or Ann Landers. The letter can be signed "Confused," "Frustrated," or with any name other than the real one.

After everyone has finished, collect the papers and redistribute them so that everyone has someone else's letter. Each person now becomes Abby or Ann Landers and writes a helpful answer or solution to the problem they were given. Allow plenty of time for this. When the answers are completed, collect the papers once again.

Now read the letters to the group one at a time, along with the answers. Discuss them, asking the group whether or not the advice given was good or bad. Other solutions to the problem can be suggested by the group. There is an excellent chance that the kids will be able to give sincere, sensible, and practical help to each other.

English Test

The following exercise is a fun way to show kids how we often make judgments too hastily. Pass out copies of the following paragraph and have each person make the corrections as instructed. Most will blow it every time. When they are finished, follow up with a discussion on Matthew 7:1-6.

Divide this paragraph into sentences using capitals at the beginning, periods at the end of sentences, and commas, etc., where needed. Once begun, DO NOT GO BACK and try to correct.

He is a young man yet experienced in vice and wickedness he is never found in opposing the works of iniquity he takes delight in the downfall of his neighbors he never rejoices in the prosperity of his fellow-creatures he is always ready to assist in destroying the peace of society he takes no pleasure in serving the Lord he is uncommonly diligent in sowing discord among his friends and acquaintances he takes no pride in laboring to promote the cause of Christianity he has not been negligent in endeavoring to tear down the church he makes no effort to subdue his evil passions he strives hard to build up Satan's kingdom he lends no aid to the support of the gospel among heathen he contributes largely to the devil he will never go to heaven he must go where he will receive his just reward.

Here is the way it should be corrected.

He is a young man, yet experienced. In vice and wickedness, he is never found. In opposing the works of iniquity, he takes delight. In the downfall of his neighbors, he never rejoices. In the prosperity of his fellow-creatures, he is always ready to assist. In destroying the peace of society, he takes no pleasure. In serving the Lord, he is uncommonly diligent. In sowing discord among his friends and acquaintances, he takes no pride. In laboring to promote the cause of Christianity, he has not been negligent. In endeavoring to tear down the church, he makes no effort. To subdue his evil passions, he strives hard. To build up Satan's kingdom, he lends no aid. To the support of the gospel among heathen, he contributes largely. To the devil he will never go. To heaven he must go, where he will receive his just reward.

Give and Get Game

Have everyone reach into their pocket or purse and produce a small amount of change (coins). Any amount will do. It works best when people use real money, but you could furnish money for them if they don't have any, or you could use play money. The game involves three rounds. Each round lasts one minute.

The first round is a *giving* round. Announce that when the signal is given, the kids should simply try to give away as much money as they can. The second round is a *getting* round. During this round, each person should try to get as much money as possible. There are no restraints on how you do this. The third round is optional. It can be either a *giving* or *getting* round. Let them vote with a show of hands and then do whichever they decide.

After this short but active game, there will be lots of possibilities for discussion. Sample questions are:

1. How many came out ahead? How many lost money in the game?

2. Which round did you enjoy the most? Why?
3. How did you feel during the *getting* round? During the *giving* round?
4. Did *greed* enter into the game?
5. Did you place a limit on how much you were going to give?
6. Did you have a strategy for getting?
7. What did you learn about giving from this game?

The Gossip Game

The Scriptures have a great deal to say about the consequences of idle gossip or "murdering with the tongue." The following game is useful as a way of pointing out the seriousness of spreading rumors.

Choose three young people to leave the room while a fourth person copies (as best he can) on poster board a picture that he is shown.

One of the three persons outside comes in and draws the same drawing, using the first person's drawing as the guide, rather than the original.

The next person comes in and draws his drawing from the second person's, and likewise with the last person.

The last person's drawing is then compared with the original, and of course, there will hardly be any resemblance to the original at all, since each of the young people copied each other, and everyone changes their drawing a little, usually omitting or adding important things.

This game is entertaining as well as revealing, and it can be followed up with a discussion on gossip and communication.

The Great Button Controversy

As a discussion starter on conformity, put one or two buttons in a box and pass them around the group. Have each student count the buttons and remember how many were in the box. By prior arrangement, the next-to-last person removes one button from the box secretly, so that the last person's count is off by one. When you ask the kids how many they counted, everyone will agree except for that one person (hopefully). In all probability, the last person will change his count to conform to the others, even though he is sure he is right. Follow up with a discussion of group pressure and how we often deny our personal convictions in order to be accepted by the group.

Interchurch Espionage

The following is a simulation game designed to teach the internal unity possible among members of the body of Christ. The game is set up as a fun thing, the players being unaware that the game has been rigged to teach a profound truth. Although the instructions are somewhat elaborate, this is only to disguise the simplicity of the game. Here's how it works.

Before the game, prepare enough slips of paper to enable everyone in the crowd to have one. Select about four sets of numbers, such as:

53	121	207	129
219	107	21	101
21	49	119	47
107	123	53	123

Fold the papers and shuffle them so they are all mixed up. The important thing is that all the number sets add up to the same sum. (In this case, 400.) The players are unaware of this, of course. Next, get enough pennies for everyone to have one, because part of the game involves flipping coins. Also have golf pencils on hand for everyone who needs one.

Explain the game to the crowd as follows: "You are all spies. In a moment you will receive a slip of paper with numbers on it. By adding the numbers, you will know the code number of the country you are spying for. The person next to you could be an enemy spy or he might be a friend from your country. You don't know. Don't reveal your code number until you have to, and make sure you add the numbers correctly. The object of the game is to: (a) eliminate enemy spies from the game, (b) locate and team up with your fellow spies, and (c) avoid being eliminated from the game. In other words, whichever country survives without being eliminated is the winner.

"You will also receive a coin and a pencil. When the game begins, add up your numbers and write the total on the paper. Next, go up to any person in the room. One of you calls 'odd,' one 'even.' Flip your coins. If they both turn up the same, whoever called 'even' is the aggressor and the other person is the responder. If the two coins turn up different (one heads and one tails), whoever called 'odd' becomes the aggressor.

"After you determine who the aggressor is, the aggressor asks, 'Friend or foe?' The responder must then show his code number. If it is the same as the aggressor's the responder remains in the game because he is a friendly spy and on the same team. He joins the aggressor by holding on to his waist and following behind. If the responder's code number is different from the aggressor's, the responder is out of the game.

"At this point, if you are still in the game, you find other survivors and the process is repeated. If you have a fellow spy behind you, then you work as a group. You are the spokesman for the group, however, if you were the original aggressor. You approach another individual or group, flip coins, and you will either eliminate, be eliminated, or form a larger group. Keep this procedure going until only one group is left. This will be the winning country."

Then play the game. Make sure there is enough room for the snakelike groups to form and move about. Of course, as the game progresses, no one will be eliminated and all will be absorbed into one long group. Try to keep the game going. The players will wise up to the fact that there aren't any enemy spies before the game is completely over. It doesn't take long for the game to be played.

After the game, discuss what happened:
1. What did you assume about the game that wasn't true? (That there were different countries, when actually there was only one.)

2. If you had known ahead of time that there weren't any enemy spies how would it have affected your play? (Probably wouldn't have been threatened, therefore no need to compete or be suspicious of others.)

Hopefully, some of the following points can be applied to this game.

1. We are all members of the same team, but often we forget and are threatened by the unknown responses of others.
2. As Christians we are all members of one body (1 Cor. 12), yet we have fractured it on all levels (denominations, cliques).
3. On a broader scale, we are all members of the family of man. We should seek to understand others better and learn to live in harmony.

The Labor Game

This game is based on the parable of the householder (Matt. 20:1-16). This sometimes perplexing story can become real by allowing your youth to experience the frustration of the workers who complained about equal pay at the end of the day, even though some did not work as long or as hard as others. The owner (God) was just and kept his promise—paying exactly what He said He would. This would have satisfied the workers until greed crept in. The following simulation game will help kids to understand this parable more fully.

As the kids enter the room, have various puzzles, brainteasers, or skills displayed on several tables. Some should be very easy, others impossible. Have points for each puzzle—depending on the difficulty, and each person is to keep his own score. After twenty or thirty minutes call a halt. Go to each young person, ask how many points he or she has, and then reach into a bag and give him a prize. The prize can be very small, just be sure every prize is exactly the same for everyone.

As you do this, it will soon be obvious to everyone in the group what is happening. No matter how high or low the score, they are all receiving equal payment. Allow free talk as you distribute the reward. Follow by discussion, prodding with questions such as "How do you honestly feel?"; "What is your attitude toward the prize-giver?"; "How do you feel toward the other young people?" Ask the person who scored the highest and the person who scored the lowest how they feel. Follow by reading the Scripture account of the parable and discuss greed, envy, lust, and competition and how these things can foul up one's relationship with God.

Star Power

This simulation game is one of the best commercially produced games on the market. It involves trading chips of different value in order to acquire as much wealth as possible. After each round of trading, those people with the most wealth form a unit and are rewarded by being allowed to change the rules of the game in any way they choose. Everyone else must abide by their new rules. The results are very interesting as the rich grow richer and the poor become very frustrated. Available from Simile II, 1150 Silverado, La Jolla, CA 92037.

Yellow Brick Road

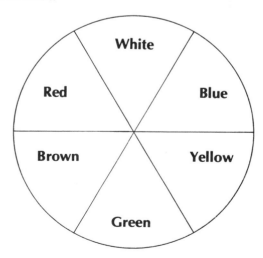

This is a very effective simulation game that teaches the balance between *competition* and *cooperation*. To play the game, a map must be made on the playing area. (It should be marked on the floor and be about twenty feet in diameter.)

Divide the group into six smaller groups and assign each a color (one of the six on the map). Each group gets a paintbrush fastened to a three-foot-long stick and some tempera paint to match the color assigned them. The following instructions are given to the players:

1. The job of your group is to build roads to the outside edge of the map. You build roads by painting them on the map in your color. The group with the most roads when the game ends, is the winner.

2. You can build roads on your own property. To make points, roads will only count if they start at your property and end at the outside edge of the map in another's property.

3. You cannot speak to anyone outside your group. Only your leader can talk to the leader of other groups. Your leader must receive permission from a group to enter its property to build a road. This must be done each time you want to build a road or branch. You must ask permission every time you cross another group's road, even in your own property. Your leader must have approval from everyone in your group before giving permission to another group.

4. A leader and painter are elected each round. Leaders cannot paint roads. Painters cannot talk to anyone, only follow directions of the leader.

5. There is no time limit. The game can end anytime. You must solve your own problems. The only people allowed on the map is the group leader and the group painter. No one else.

After the game has ended, discuss what happened. Let each person express feelings experienced during the game. Compare these feeling to what we feel in real-life situations as we work closely with others.

For example, you might ask, What does the game say about the nature of man? On what basis were decisions and bargains made? How much hostility was there? Should any of the rules of the game be changed?

Learning By Being Creative

Junior highers can be very creative when they are given the opportunity, and they can learn much about their faith by expressing it creatively in many ways.

Some kids enjoy writing; others are into music, art, or dramatics. Even when a person doesn't have natural talent, he can enjoy the experience of just being creative in his own way.

The creative arts can be used very effectively in all kinds of learning experiences. Next time you discuss the concept of "God," for instance, have the kids do something other than just talk or hear about God. Give them felt-tipped pens and have them draw a picture of what they imagine God looks like, or write a song about Him, or paste together a collage of magazine clippings that illustrate the nature of God. Then allow each person to share their creation with the entire group. You can do it with almost any topic and in any form of expression. Kids are forced to think about things in a little different way and the results are amazing. The following idea is just an example of what can be done.

Love Groups

This exercise is a five-session project designed for more informal times with your junior high group. The basic purpose is to let the kids be creative and imaginative about the subject of Christian love through many different activities. The teacher or youth leader acts as a traffic director and organizer and supplies very little lecture-type teaching.

The basic format of the five sessions has each person working in an activity group for the first four sessions. Each of these activity groups is working on something directly related to the subject of Christian love. During the class period (while the activity groups are working), the leader stops all the groups for one of a variety of give-and-take sessions that include minilectures (3 minutes), discussion, a short film, or whatever, all dealing with the subject of love. The fifth session is devoted to presentation of each of the activity groups' finished products. (For example, the drama group would present their drama, and the "love banners" group would auction off their banners, etc.) Adults or other youth groups can be invited to the fifth session to see and hear the presentations. Kids select a group from among the selections below, according to their interests and abilities:

1. *The Signs of Love Slide Show:* This group will shoot pictures of signs of love all around them, have them developed, and create a slide show with narration or music.
2. *Drama:* This group will prepare a play on some facet of Christian love. It can be original or it can be a well-known Bible story.
3. *The Crossword Puzzle Group:* This group will design one or more crossword puzzles based on the subject of Christian love.
4. *The Poetry Group:* This group will write poetry about Christian love.
5. *The Cartoon Group:* This group will publish a booklet of Christian love cartoons. They can be original or from other publications.
6. *The Bible Scholar Group:* This group will research the concept of Christian love in the Scriptures using commentaries, other books, etc., and write a report on their findings.
7. *The Love Banner Group:* This group must have some artistic and sewing abilities, because they will produce banners on the subject of Christian love.
8. *The Songwriting Group:* This group will compose Christ-

ian love songs and perform them. They can be completely original or new words to familar tunes.

9. *The Love Object Group:* This group will produce love-related art objects to auction off or give away, such as love necklaces, plaques, calligraphy, paintings, or whatever.

Each group should be supplied with the necessary items to complete their work and the kids should be encouraged to work at home on their project as well. This basic format could be used with other topics as well, and other special interest groups could be added to meet the needs of your group.

Learning Outside the Classroom

Many times it is extremely helpful to take junior highers on field trips to enhance learning. Learning involves a great deal more than just hearing information. We also learn by seeing, touching, smelling, and so on. Whenever you can give kids the opportunity to experience life more fully, taking advantage of all the senses, it is going to make a greater impression. Here are a couple of good ideas that put this concept into practice.

The Poor Man's Holy Land Tour

You can have a Holy Land tour without actually going there, simply by escorting your junior highers to places within walking or driving distance that resemble biblical locations. This could include taking them to the tallest building in town and having a Bible study there about Satan tempting Jesus to jump from the high mountain. It might also include a trip to the city jail where you could talk about Paul's imprisonment. The options are endless: a Jewish synagogue, a mountainside (for the Sermon on the Mount), a garden (for the Garden of Gethsemane), an upstairs room (for the Last Supper), an old boiler room (for the story of the Hebrew children in the fiery furnace), on a country road (for the story of Paul's Damascus road experience), a lakefront, or a wilderness area (depending on where you live). Doing something like this as a visual aid is worth a thousand flannelgraphs.

A *Tour of Your Life*

This day-long field trip is great with junior highs and gives them an opportunity to view life somewhat more completely and realistically. Begin by visiting the maternity ward of a local hospital (prearranged, of course) where the kids can see newborns and their parents. Perhaps a doctor can tell about the birth process. Next, take the kids to a local college or university campus and show them around. The next stop should be a factory or shop. At this point, the need for work and the types of work available can be discussed.

Then visit with older folks in a convalescent home or some other place where senior citizens live. Allow the kids to share with them in some way and allow the seniors to also share with the kids. The last stop on the tour should be a mortuary or funeral home. The funeral director may show the kids around, explain what happens to the corpse when it is brought in, the types of caskets available, and so on. Close the experience with a meeting or discussion in the funeral chapel (if there is one) or elsewhere if you wish. Other places can be added to this tour depending on how much time you have or the types of places available to you. Allow kids to think about the kind of life they want, and how they are going to achieve their goals.

Learning About Values

Junior highers are involved in a constant process of clarifying their values and beliefs. Many of their values are fragile and temporary. Since most day-to-day decisions are based on the values that an individual holds, it is important for kids to be able to identify their values and to know why they hold them.

Values Clarification: A Handbook of Practical Strategies for Teachers and Students by Sidney B. Simon, Leland W. Howe, and Howard Kirschenbaum is an excellent resource for values clarification theory and ideas. According to the authors, something cannot really be considered a value unless it has been (1) *chosen* freely from alternatives, and after consideration of the consequences; (2) *prized* (cherished) and publicly affirmed; and (3) *acted upon*, with repitition and consistency.[2] Most values clarification strategies are simply exercises that force people to think about, to question, and to evaluate what they believe (or think they believe) on a given subject. They are never ends in themselves; they should lead to discussion and discovery. When used in the church, they help kids to see how their faith relates to their values and how the gospel affects what they believe.

Whenever leading junior highers through strategies like the ones suggested here, be sure to allow each person the freedom to express his or her opinion without criticism or judgment. Create an atmosphere of openness. There is never a "right answer" when you are asking kids to share what they believe or think. If they are being honest, then they are giving the best answer they could possibly give. Even if they are way off-base according to your values or the values of the church, it is important that they be allowed to express themselves openly. Allow kids to come up with some "right answers" on their own. A good discussion should be a cooperative search for truth, and you as the discussion leader (as well as participant) should encourage each person to explore the subject matter as thoroughly as possible, so that they might gain better insights into what they (and others) believe.

Decision

Give each person five or ten minutes to decide which of the following things they consider to be the most harmful. Their job is to rank each item by writing the number 1 by the thing they think is the most harmful; number 2 by the second most harmful, etc. Afterward, discuss the results. Define "harmful" as it relates to all areas of life.

_____Getting drunk
_____Moderate drinking (alcohol)
_____Lack of exercise
_____Cigarette smoking

_____Not going to church
_____Poor eating habits (types of food, how eaten, etc.)
_____Marijuana
_____Drugs (amphetamines, LSD, etc.)
_____Watching too much TV
_____Lack of medical attention when necessary
_____Premarital sex
_____Nervous anxiety and tension
_____Fatigue, caused by never getting enough sleep
_____Overeating
_____Cheating on exams at school

Foto-Match

Hang up twenty or so photos of people (all kinds—old, young, black, white, attractive, ugly, fat, slim, wealthy, poor). The first week the pictures are displayed, have the kids write descriptions of each person based on what they see in the picture. Collect them all and during the following week, combine all the individual descriptions into a concise paragraph that accurately reflects the group consensus. Attach the descriptions to each picture for the next meeting. Have the students look at the photos and the descriptions carefully (make sure they are numbered) and then answer the following questions:

1. Choose five people you would want to work with for one year. Why?
2. Is there any one person you would not want anything to do with? Why?
3. Who, if any, would you be willing to go out with on a date?
4. Who, if any, would you worship with?
5. Which person do you think you could really like? Why?
6. If only five others and yourself were allowed to live and the others executed, which five would stay with you? Why?

You could have your group go through the questions again and perhaps decide how their parents would respond. And, of course, you can easily come up with other questions equally as good as these.

How God Sees Me

Each person is asked to take a sheet of newsprint and on one side draw pictures, cartoons, or sayings expressing "How I See God." The other side is to be filled with symbols expressing "How I Think God Sees Me." Allow twenty to twenty-five minutes to complete. After everyone is finished, each person should explain their drawing to the entire group. This exercise opens a group up to sharing where each one stands with God at present and demonstrates the varying facets of an individual's experience with God.

Human Continuum

When discussing subjects that have many points of view, have the kids arrange themselves (prior to the discussion) on a human continuum from one extreme viewpoint to the opposite extreme. For example, if you are discussing drinking, have the kids line up with all those are are for drinking on one end, and those who are against it at the other. Undecideds or moderates would be somewhere in the middle.

For	Against

Kids may discuss the issue among themselves as they attempt to find the right spot in the line in relationship to each other. After they are settled, further discussion or debate can take place as kids attempt to defend their positions. Anyone may change positions at any time.

Lamed Vovnik Convention

A charming Jewish legend states that the world exists due to the presence of only thirty-six righteous people. The Jewish name for these people is *lamed vov* (pronounced "lahmed vov")—"thirty-six." These people may be of any station in life, poor or mighty, men or women, hermits or public figures. The only thing we know about them is that they are alive and that they do not know that they are lamed vovniks. If they claim to be, then they cannot be.

To conduct a lamed vovnik convention, divide your group into as many small groups as you wish, and have each group nominate several individuals whom they think might qualify as a lamed vovnik. They should be righteous, selfless, and the kind of persons on whom the welfare of the world might rest. Each group should take ten to fifteen minutes for this. Set a maximum number of people that each group may nominate.

When the groups have finished, have a nominating convention. Each group announces its choices and explains why they nominated whom they did. A list can be kept on a blackboard, and a final vote can be taken to arrive at the entire group's guesses at who the thirty-six lamed vovniks are.

Many famous people will undoubtedly be nominated, but the beauty of the exercise is that many ordinary people, not well-known, will undoubtedly be favorites. Perhaps the best thing about the activity is the shift of emphasis from fame to humility. True models begin to emerge and kids begin to put some handles on what righteousness is all about.

Life Auction

Print up or display the following list of life options and give each person an equal amount of money (play money or poker chips). Then have an auction, in which the kids try to acquire as many of the items on the list as they feel they want and can afford. Once their money is gone, they can bid on nothing else. Give the kids time to decide and set their priorities before the bidding begins. You can add other items to the list if necessary. If you have more kids then items, sell each item twice. Or have the kids get into small groups, decide what they want, and then bid in groups. It's a great way to get into a discussion on what is important in life and what is not.

Life Options

1. A wonderful family life without any hassles.
2. All the money I need to be happy.
3. Never to be sick.
4. To find the right mate, who is good-looking and fulfills me.
5. Never to have pimples.
6. To be able to do whatever I want whenever I want.
7. To have all the power the president has.
8. To be the best-looking person in the world.
9. To have a real hunger to read the Bible faithfully.
10. To be able to understand all things.
11. To eliminate all hunger and disease in the world.
12. To always be close to God.
13. Never to feel lonely or put down.
14. Always be happy and peaceful.
15. Never feel hurt.
16. To own a beautiful home, car, boat, plane, and seven motorcycles—one for each day of the week.
17. To be supersmart without ever having to attend school.
18. To be able to excel quickly and to be superior in all things.
19. To be filled with God's presence in the most dynamic way.
20. To always know that you are in God's will.
21. To be the greatest athlete in the world.
22. To be looked up to by everyone else.
23. To become a star on TV.
24. To always have a lot of close friends who never let you down.
25. To walk close to God.

Life Letters

Following a discussion of suicide, have kids write a life letter to a potential suicide victim expressing their reasons for believing that life is worth living. After about twenty minutes of writing, have the kids share their letters with the rest of the group (if they want to). This gives some people a chance to share their faith and provide a unique learning experience as well.

The Moral of the Story

Read a story (proverb, fable, biblical, or make-believe) and leave out the moral at the end, if there is one. Challenge each person to write down what they think the moral of the story could be. They can then share them and discuss. It's amazing how many different things you can learn from one simple story.

Perfect Pair

For a good discussion starter on the family, try this one. Simply tell kids that they are to invent the world's most perfect couple; that is, the man and woman best suited to create the ideal home and family and most likely to be happy. Divide into small groups and have them describe their perfect couple. Things to consider:

1. The couple themselves
   a. background
   b. age
   c. education
   d. religious affiliation
   e. race
   f. political views
2. Their life style
   a. jobs (employment)
   b. hobbies
   c. sex life
   d. leisure time
   e. entertainment
   f. habits
   g. friends and associations
3. Their possessions
   a. money
   b. furniture
   c. house and neighborhood
   d. books, magazines

    e. appliances
    f. recreational needs
    g. auto(s)
4. Philosophy on child rearing
    a. discipline
    b. education
    c. manners
    d. dress
    e. independence

The items listed are only suggestions and kids should not be limited to them. After a twenty- or thirty-minute period of working in their groups, have each describe their perfect couple. Make lists on the blackboard or on an overhead projector. Compare each group's description of their couple.

Discuss the differences and similarities and ask why certain characteristics occur more often than others. Talk about prejudices and relate to Scripture. What matters and what doesn't? Also discuss the interaction that took place in each small group—the disputes, differences of opinion, and so forth. You can get a lot of healthy discussion out of this exercise.

Quickies

One easy way to get kids to open up and to express themselves on a particular topic is to give them "quickies"—"finish this sentence" phrases they must respond to. They can either be written out by each person secretly on cards, passed in (without names, of course) and read back to the group by the leader, or they can be discussed in small groups. If you use the latter method, have the kids get into groups of four and share their answers with each other, one at a time. It's not only a good way to get kids thinking, but it also encourages communication among group members. Allow kids the freedom to pass if a question is too hard to answer. Here are a few sample quickies that you might be able to use:

1. I am proud of . . .
2. I wish I were . . .
3. I wish I were not . . .
4. I wish I had . . .
5. I wish I had not . . .
6. I wish I could . . .
7. I fear most . . .
8. My favorite place is . . .
9. I wish my parents would . . .
10. If I had a hundred dollars, I would . . .
11. I hate . . .
12. My hero is . . .
13. The hardest thing for me to do is . . .
14. I am really happy when . . .
15. If I were God, I would . . .

Role Bowl

Print up the following situations on cards and put them in a bowl. Divide into small groups and let each person pick one out and think about it. Ask the kids to share their solutions to the situation. (The more verbal kids will obviously share first. *But don't force anyone to share!*) After each person finishes, allow others in the group to comment or add their own thoughts.

1. I don't get it. If Christianity is true, how come there are so many religions that call themselves Christian? I mean, what's the difference between Baptists, Presbyterians, and all the others?
2. If you ask me, the Christian religion makes you a "doormat"—always loving and turning the other cheek.
3. What if I lived like a nonbeliever for eighty years and then became a Christian on my deathbed? Would Billy Graham and I go to the same place?
4. I have been reading through the Old Testament for English class. How come God ordered his people to kill everybody—even women and children—when they conquered a land? What kind of a God is that?

5. Your mother and I do not believe in all this Jesus stuff and we think you spend too much time in church. So we want you to stay away from church for a while.
6. If God is God, then how come you can't see him or it? Why don't you prove that God exists? Go ahead . . . prove it to me.
7. The Bible has some nice little stories in it, but everyone knows it's full of contradictions, errors, and just plain myths. How can you believe it?
8. I know a bunch of people who go to your church and they are supposed to be Christians, but I also know what they do during the week and at parties that I go to. They are phonies. If Christianity is so great, how come so many phonies?
9. My little brother died of leukemia and I prayed like crazy. Don't tell me there is a God who loves us. How come he didn't help my brother?
10. Look, I know I am overweight and even though it hurts me to say it, I'm ugly. And I started coming to your church because I thought the kids in your youth group would treat me differently than the kids at school. Wrong! They ignore me and make fun of me just like everyone else. How come?

Run for Your Life

Although this strategy deals with the subject of death, it is really about life and how we live it. The purpose of this exercise is to help young people to evaluate their priorities in light of what is really important. It allows the group to contrast what they are doing now with what they would do if they had only one month to live. Give each person in the group a list similar to the one below.

If I only had one month to live, I would:
1. perform some high-risk feat that I have always wanted to do, figuring that if I don't make it, it won't really matter.
2. stage an incredible robbery for a large amount of money,

which I would immediately give to the needy and starving of the world.
3. not tell anyone.
4. use my dilemma to present the gospel to as many people as I could.
5. spend all my time in prayer and Bible reading.
6. make my own funeral arrangements.
7. offer myself to science or medicine for high-risk experiments.
8. have as much fun as possible (sex, parties, booze, whatever turns me on).
9. travel around the world and see as much as possible.
10. buy lots of stuff on credit that I've always wanted: expensive cars, fancy clothes, exotic food. ("Sorry, the deceased left no forwarding address.")
11. spend my last month with my family or close personal friends.
12. not do anything much different; just go on as always.
13. isolate myself from everyone; find a remote place and meditate.
14. write a book about my life (or last month).
15. sell all my possessions and give the money to my family, friends, or others who need it.
16. try to accomplish as many worthwhile projects as possible.
17. _____.

Have the group rank these alternatives (plus any they wish to add). The first item on their list would be the one they would most likely do, and the last would be the one they would least likely do. Have everyone share their choices, explain why they chose that way, and then discuss the results with the entire group. Another way to evaluate the alternatives is to put each one on a continuum. One end of the continuum would be "Yes, definitely" and the other end would be "Absolutely not." After each alternative is placed on the continuum, compare and discuss with the rest of the group.

Space Capsule

This exercise is to help kids determine how they place value on human life and human characteristics. Even though this is a tough task and extremely hypothetical, it is good for kids to be forced to make some value judgments such as this once in a while, just to get a handle on what they believe.

Set it up this way: You announce that the world is about to be involved in a nuclear war, and it is expected that the entire population of the world will be destroyed. (Never mind the impossibility of this or the theology involved.) Scientists have prepared ten people, selected at random, to escape this disaster by being shot into outer space in a space capsule for three months. They will return after the holocaust to begin re-populating the earth once again. The ten people are (you can change this list):

1. An accountant, about 30
2. His pregnant wife, 28
3. A girl in college, 18
4. A famous female movie star, 28
5. A pro basketball player, 24
6. A male medical student, 25
7. A famous female novelist, 43
8. A Catholic priest, 70
9. An armed policeman, 32
10. The policeman's wife, a biochemist, 30

Unfortunately, a problem came up at the last moment: It was discovered that the capsule would hold only six people, not ten. The job of the group now is to decide which four people must be left behind. Discuss in small groups and have the kids give good reasons for their decisions. Many issues will surface.

Ten Years From Now

Here's a fun exercise to get kids thinking about the future. Print the following on a half sheet of paper and let the kids answer away. Don't have them put their name on the paper (if your group is shy) and discuss the answers as a group. If your kids don't mind sharing their responses then simply go around the group and discuss each one individually.

Ten Years From Now . . .

1. My height: _____
2. My weight: _____
3. My hair style: _____
4. Where I will be living: _____
5. What I will be doing: _____
6. Dreams and goals I will have: _____
7. I feel I will have been a success in life if . . .
8. I will look back on this year as a year of . . .

Service Projects

Junior highers need to be given opportunities to express their faith in practical and meaningful ways. They also need to feel the sense of accomplishment and self-worth that comes from serving others and from getting involved in worthwhile activities that demonstrate to others the love of Christ. Service projects like the ones that follow work very well with junior highers to help fulfill those needs. They are especially good because they do not require long-term commitments from the kids, which often tend to frustrate them. These projects may be accomplished in a relatively short period of time and with good results.

It is important for junior highers to understand that the gospel is not just words, but also action. Too often love is talked about in the church without the necessary emphasis on doing it. Service projects are simple yet practical ways to help kids to put a handle on their faith and to turn Christian love into real, significant action. Junior highers are fully capable of following through on them and usually will get very excited about the possibilities.

The following games are just a few of the many possibilities for putting faith into action.

Adopt-a-Garden

Here's an idea that can really "grow" on you: Invite your group to adopt the gardens of shut-in, chronically ill, hospitalized, or aged people. Supply the seeds and encourage the youth to supply the tools and muscle power. They can prepare the soil, plant, cultivate, and ultimately harvest the vegetables for the people who own the gardens and who, of course, are unable to do the work. It makes for great interaction between the generations! Especially helpful are youth who are into farming, biology, and the "back-to-the-earth" movement.
An adaptation of this idea involves others in the congregation. While publicizing "Adopt-a-Garden," invite others who already have gardens to set aside one or two rows for giving the harvest to the hungry. Again, youth can supply the seeds, and after the harvest, can deliver the food to the needy. This can fit well into a long-range hunger-awareness program.

Convalescent Home Ministry

Arrange with one or more of the convalescent homes in your area for a group of junior highers to come in and minister in some way to the patients on a regular basis. As a group, the kids can put on special programs or they may minister in a more direct way, such as by reading to people who have lost much of their vision, helping them to write letters, feeding them, or similar tasks as directed by the convalescent home director. Most convalescent homes welcome this kind of involvement by youth groups and, of course, the experience is a valuable one for the kids. If you have a home for retarded children in your area, the same kind of ministry can be done there. Junior highers should to be exposed to people who are less fortunate in order to develop a healthy concern and respect for them.

Golf Club Washing

Here's a unique fund raiser that gets good results. Set up a booth at the eighteenth green of a local golf course and offer to wash golf clubs for the tired hackers. All you need is permission from the golf course pro (or park board for municipal courses), a pail of soapy water, a brush, a pail of clean water, a coin collector, and a few towels. For extra service, you may want to wax the woods and use metal polish on the irons. When the money is going to a worthy cause, most golfers will be glad to pay a reasonable price.

Group Garage Sales

Garage sales are big business these days. There are actually professional garage sale shoppers who do nothing but hit all the sales in town each week looking for bargains. Invite the people in the congregation to donate all kinds of unwanted but sellable items to the junior high group and then borrow someone's garage for a Saturday and have a garage sale. Put an ad in the local paper, and post lots of signs pointing people to the sale. Price each item low enough that it will sell easily, and the results will be surprising. The money can then be used for a worthy cause of your choosing.

Let It Growl

This is a combination "Lock In" and "Starve-a-thon" designed to raise money for Third World countries and to sensitize kids to the problem of world hunger. The group meets together on a Friday evening and remains together until the following evening, participating in a fast—going without food for at least twenty-four hours. During this time, there are many games, simulations, films, and other activities that can be used to focus on the hunger issue. The kids are also encouraged to obtain sponsors prior to the event; the sponsor pays a certain amount of money (as much as possible) for each hour the person is able to go without food. The money is then collected and contributed to a relief agency that is helping to supply food to undernourished people around the world.

One relief agency, World Vision (919 W. Huntington Drive, Monrovia, Calif. 91016), has creatively organized this program and has it ready to go for your youth group—including pledge cards for the sponsors, posters, "Let It Growl" buttons and T-shirts, and so on. They will also furnish free films and suggest other activities to help make the event a success.

An Over-65 Party

Have the junior highers throw a party for the senior citizens of the community. Play games, serve refreshments, sing old songs the old-timers know, and do things with them, rather than just having them watch. It makes the old folks feel a little younger, helps the kids to learn to appreciate the elderly, and makes a great service project.

Rake and Run

Here's a great way to involve junior highers in a ministry to the community, if you live in a neighborhood with a lot of trees. Load up all the kids in a bus and "arm" each with a lawn rake. You just go up and down streets and whenever you see a lawn that needs raking, everyone jumps out and rakes all the leaves up. No pay is accepted for any of the work. It is all done in the name of Christ. You might find out the names of shut-ins who cannot rake their own lawns. It can be fun and rewarding for the kids. Note: During the winter, kids can shovel snow in the same way. You can call it "Snow and Blow."

Rockathon

Here's a fun idea that involves everyone in the group and serves as a great service project, too. It's a twenty-four hour rockathon. Each participant signs up sponsors for twenty-five cents (or more) for every hour he rocks on his rocking chair. Here are the rules:
1. Everyone provides their own rocking chair.
2. Each participant must rock at least four hours in succession.
3. Time breaks allowed only for trips to the bathroom.
4. The chair must be moving at all times.

Hold the event in a large room and supply plenty of TVs, record players, radios, coffee, cookies, and lemonade. Keep the participants awake by cheering, and a lot of cold, wet towels. Meals can be provided by the church, families, or whatever. After participants finish rocking, they are given an official time certificate to show their sponsor. Keep a master record on all participants and their times to make sure each sponsor's money is collected. Take a lot of pictures, advertise it well in advance, and invite spectators. Also, keep track of the total amount of money raised and announce it to the kids every four or five hours. It keeps enthusiasm high. The money can then be donated to a worthy cause of the group's choosing.

Scavenger Food Hunt

This game is fun, and it can also make a significant contribution to a poor family or families in your local area. It's especially good around Thanksgiving. The group is divided into teams and is given a list of canned goods or other food items they are to try to collect from homes within a specified area. The group that collects the most items on the list is the winner, but the real winners are the people who receive the donated food. Each home that contributes should receive a thank-you note, which can also serve as a receipt. It is best to work through a local welfare agency or other organization that can help with the distribution of the food.

The Supermarket Blitz

Here's another way to collect food for needy families. Station a small group of kids outside the entrances to supermarkets in the area. (Get permission first.) The kids should have large containers in which canned goods or other food items can be deposited. The kids ask people going into the store if they would purchase one extra item of their choice to be donated to a needy family in the area. Make sure the people know that a legitimate church or other agency is involved in the food distribution program, and give receipts to those who desire them. It's a pretty effective way to collect food and to help others in Christ's name.

Notes

[1]Findley Edge, *The Greening of the Church* (Waco, Texas: Word Books, 1971), pp. 168-69.
[2]Sidney B. Simon, Leland W. Howe, and Howard Kirschenbaum, *Values Clarification: A Handbook of Practical Strategies for Teachers and Students* (New York: Hart Publishing Co., 1972), p. 36.

Suggested Resources

Peter Blos, *The Young Adolescent* (New York: The Free Press, 1970).

Robert Browning, *Communicating with Junior Highs* (Nashville, Tenn.: Graded Press, 1968).

Arnold Gesell, Frances L. Ilg, and Louise B. Ames, *Youth: The Years From Ten to Sixteen* (New York: Harper and Row, 1956).

Ginny Ward Holderness, *The Exuberant Years* (Atlanta: John Knox Press, 1976).

Peter Mayle, *What's Happening to Me? A Guide to Puberty* (Secancus, New Jersey: Lyle Stuart, Inc., 1975).

Lynn Minton, *Growing Into Adolescence* (New York: Parent's Magazine Press, 1972).

Wayne Rice and Mike Yaconelli, *Way-Out Ideas for Youth Groups* (Grand Rapids, Mich.: Zondervan Publishing, 1972).

Wayne Rice and Mike Yaconelli, *Right-On Ideas for Youth Groups* (Grand Rapids, Mich.: Zondervan Publishing, 1973).

Wayne Rice and Mike Yaconelli, *Far-Out Ideas for Youth Groups* (Grand Rapids, Mich.: Zondervan Publishing, 1975).

Fr. Richard Reichert, "Prime Time" (2 cassettes on junior high ministry), N.C.R. Cassettes, P.O. Box 281, Kansas City, Mo. 64141.